REVOLUTIONARY ALCHEMY

REVOLUTIONARY ALCHEMY

Collected Poems
1967 - 2012

John Curl

Some of these poems have appeared in the following anthologies, periodicals, and online zines:

Poetry USA, Oakland Out Loud, Walk Upon The Waters, Amerus, Third Rail, Blake Times, The Unrealist, Soup, What is Real?, Peace Or Perish, Left Curve, Sparks of Fire, Merlyn Gorky, Clay Drum, Love Lights, Pulse of the People, THE, Toward Revolutionary Art, Haight-Ashbury Literary Quarterly, City Arts, Anthology of East Bay Poets, Foolkiller, Poetalk, Radical America, The Circle, Ball, Grassroots, Berkeley Literary Review, Outlet, Oxygen, Terrain, Grist, Challenge, The Black Panther, Poetry Flash, Savoy, San Francisco Salvo, The Boa, Asphyxia, Aware, Curiosity's Escape, Downcast and Dejected on a Cloudy Day, Gopher, Idling, Red Coral, Psychozoan, Richmond Review, Real Poetic, Sparks, Butterfly Jubilee, Thunder Sandwich, Thought Monkeys, The Shallow End, Think-ink.net, Trick House, Revolutionary Poets Brigade, 100 Thousand Poets for Change.

ISBN 13: 978-0615704142

Homeward Press
P.O. Box 2755
Berkeley, CA 94702
www.red-coral.net

Cover Design: John Curl

In 1967, at age 27, I needed to be reborn, so I destroyed all my earlier work. Shortly after that I began writing again. I wrote the last section in this collection between 1967 and 1971. Most of this book is organized in a loose reverse chronology, with the more recent poems and poem cycles first. Most sections consist of a cycle that I wrote in the same general time period. But some sections do not follow that pattern, and are grouped by type, such as narrative poems or lyric poems with more personal themes. Many of these poems have appeared in magazines, ezines, and anthologies. The poems in the first section, American Antidotes, are the most recent, and this is the first time that they appear as a collection. Almost all of the other poems were published in the following chapbooks:

Scorched Birth (Beatitude Press, 2004)
Columbus in the Bay of Pigs (Homeward Press/Inkworks,1991)
Decade (Mother's Hen, 1987)
Tidal News (Homeward Press, 1982)
Cosmic Athletics (Poetry For The People, 1980)
Ride the Wind (Poetry For The People, 1979)
Spring Ritual (Cloud House, 1978)
Insurrection/Resurrection (Working People's Artists, 1975)
Commu 1 (Gnosis Press, 1971)
Change/Tears (Drop City, 1967)

CONTENTS

FOREWORD

At 79 and for most of my adult life a communist as a poet, I think I can say a few words about what makes American poetry tick (or be ticked off), and by way of that indicate the importance of this book and John Curl in the pantheon of revolutionary poets.

Poets live in the world. They have their wars. Whitman's was the Civil War. He wrote before it began and after it was over but it was the event in his life that resonates in most of his poetry.

I speak of Walt at the outset because he is the founding father of modern poetry in the western world—and I daresay even in the Eastern and African worlds as well. In the American dimension he gave birth to the great poets of the 20th century, ie., William Carlos Williams, Ezra Pound (though denied for a long time), Charles Olson, Allen Ginsberg. And certainly Jack Kerouac was born not in Lowell, Mass., but in "The Song of the Open Road"—perhaps the finest American poem ever writ.

And certainly if no Whitman, there's no Vladimir Mayakovsky or Pablo Neruda.

Here I am talking poetry, not literature, which is always after the event of the making of a poem. And in this respect, the Vietnam war was John Curl's war. When he writes in his own brief preface to *Revolutionary Alchemy: Poems 1967-2012* that "In 1967, at age 27, I needed to be reborn, so I destroyed all my earlier work" we see a very conscious awareness at work. In 1967 the Vietnam war was two years old.

When he did what he did in 1967, though he probably wasn't fully conscious of it then, he left what I call the "literary" dimension, that is, he shook off the cultural corporatism that turns out literary poets all over the States, and he entered the revolutionary realm.

That is, he began to write poetry in order to change the world.

This dimension of poetry is not talked enough about in this country, and the lack of such discourse goes hand-in-hand with refusers or deniers of revolutionary potentials.

Poets are usually thought of as writers who reflect the world, bringing in their feelings, their heartfeltness to go along with their mindfulness. Most academic literature falls into that category. It is a poetry of privileged sensitivity, verbal virtuosity, containing even hints of genius in the traditional way genius means a poet who has "lasted" through the centuries.

There is another realm of poetry however, which isn't interested at all in simply reflecting the world "as it is" to a subjectivity. In that realm there's only one thing—-and it is the foundation of all its poets—: the desire to increase revolutionary motion with poetry.

John Curl's work is a stellar embodiment of that creed.

To Curl, change is every moment.

Big change is: Revolution a-comin'.

Whether he is writing a very visual poem, describing his girlfriend, which concludes with a raunchy grabbing of her ass (to change every moment), or directly didactic, even propagandistic:

"We owe nothing to the banks
We owe nothing to the corporations"

it is "transform, transform" that John Curl is forever sounding and resounding with his depth charges. And this isn't the old transformation idea that went along with "writing a good poem." We're talking about transforming a society totally in which process poetry serves as a beaconing forward.

Curl's signature achievement linguistically, it seems to me, is to have developed a language where lines of images often are contrary to one another and that friction or opposition does more than "surrealize" the lines (Curl knows the techniques of all the avant-garde poetry movements of the 20th century)—what he is writing is often a poetry of dialectical motion itself.

The singular intent behind John's writing is to actualize in poetry the urgent need for working-class consciousness,—especially as, with the robotization and electronic replacement of workers already well on it way to creating of New Class of proletarians who will never work again or will work for menial wages and receive little or no benefits,—and Curl succeeds in so many poems and in so many imaginings in this book that one realizes that *Revolutionary Alchemy* is a book of major importance.

Already well-known as a chronicler of work co-operatives in the United States (1980) and, more recently, his *For All the People* (2009/2012), as well as the translator of Ancient American poetry from Aztec and Quechua, John Curl, a woodworker by trade and the vice-president of the Oakland, California PEN, has earned a place—with this book of poems—among the foremost revolutionary American poets since the end of WW2. When you inhabit the scope and depths of these poems, I am certain you will agree with my assessment.

Jack Hirschman

REVOLUTIONARY ALCHEMY

AMERICAN ANTIDOTES

AMERICA FIRST

Beyond the well, along the dusty road,
America first,
the acrid, rust-red soil supporting
only an occasional small vineyard,
they strolled house to house,
executing families.

We heard a great noise and
were all enveloped in a wall
of heat and steam, while
concrete balconies crashed
into parked cars, an officer
lowered a plastic bag over her
head while another ground a lit
cigarette into her arm,
America first.

The melting snow, semi-translucent
and shining in the lantern glow,
seemed to be carved out
of a block of amber.
We worked
our way back, following
a little creek, sucking on
twigs of sassafras
and radiant sunshine
until, fringed by majestic pines,
we reached the canyon edge
and lit the sacred fire.

Although the time scale was so
vast and the abuse of evidence
so complete as to render it
unlikely, the flutes
and rattles summoned a
universal healing,
America first.

It was a moment of return,

the ancient languages,
long declared extinct by the experts,
springing suddenly back to life.
All we had were elders, drums, spirits,
and what they told us.

THE AMERICAN DREAM

While bodies, some
still handcuffed, gagged,
and body parts pile up
at the morgue, colorful
bouquets
of entry and exit wounds,
lacerations, contusions,
acid burns, punctures
apparently made with an electric
drill. The filing of
serious charges
in such cases
have been rare
in the American dream.

Northern lights fire the horizon.
On an island in the green river
of the northwest valley,
on a humble plant, flowering in
early spring, a larva
molts its skin, transforming
into a nymph.

Lost dogs
and stray families
searching for food
following prophesies
prowl the night streets
of the American dream.

AN AMERICAN TRAGEDY

Two earth spirits
of the pristine forest
were killed
by trailside bombs during sunset.
The presumed bombers
apparently fled the scene
on dirt bikes
for an adjoining canyon
cracked up to be
a virtual no-man's land.

In other news,
death squads detained an
additional thirty-one math students,
security guards shot
fourteen laborers as they slept
in their pup tents,
celebrity bodyguards
dined on five civilians,
and an assistant professor
of south Asian music
harpooned two dolphins,
six yellow dogs, a mule,
an unarmed opossum,
sixteen house cats of various colors
and assorted birds.

After several commercials,
the pundits yelled
at each other
hotly debating
whether it was
a situation comedy or
an American tragedy.

THAT'S WHAT MADE AMERICA GREAT

The first day of autumn,
the gleam of sunset on the edges
of impenetrable clouds.
The d.a. hands over the deleted files
to the jackal handling
the investigation into himself,
the caliber, distance from which
the bullets were fired, and
angle of entry
proving it was the work of just
one deranged individual
who, reports confirm,
has committed suicide:
that's what made America great.

They zip the bodies into bags
and stack them neatly behind
the elegantly pruned hedges.
Ignited apparently as a distraction,
a brush fire lit by the bailiffs
on orders from the judge
burns hundreds of humble homes
and thousands of banned books
to the ground.
To assure that the rules of
global finance are favorable
to certain corporate interests,
after the barrage of seven mortar rounds,
masked men in police uniforms
grab people at random,
and herd them into waiting vans.
Suddenly, without warning,
thousands of children
in seemingly haphazard locations
defy all authority:
that's what made America great.

Sheer cliffs, stony beaches,

sandy dunes, tidal pools,
waves on a moonlit lake.
The stream bed a parched channel
of rocks and pebbles in March
without warning becomes
an unstoppable torrent in April,
spreading inexorably across
the full extent of the flood plain
into the forest.
The suddenly-moist forest floor
strewn with withered
debris of decaying trees
springs abruptly back to life.
Seed pods soak up just enough
concentrated energy, patiently wait
for the waters to subside,
for their inevitable moment in the sun.
A generation yearning for oases of normalcy
in the throes of everyday violence,
comes precipitately into maturity,
and realizes that the howling ghosts of
past defeats by the plutocracy
mean nothing
less than the call of the future
for heroes organizing resistance,
revolt, and revolution:
that's what made America great.

AMERICA THE BEAUTIFUL

Automatic weapons in the hands
of children roaming
the abandoned schools,
mortar shells striking
groups of tarred and feathered
construction workers
seeking jobs;
pillage and rape on Main Street
by orders of
the senior commanders.
How events unfolded and
who might have been involved,
conspiracy theories flying wildly about,
the entire armed services
and chambers of commerce
issuing quick robust denials,
while shivering investigators
secretly pray
the bodies are never exhumed,
America the beautiful.

To bolster the crumbling dollar
the People's Representatives
bloat the military budget
and drain social programs.
Tight-lipped judges scramble
to defuse the explosive situation,
important forensic evidence
spirited away in
heavily armed humvees,
while in broad daylight in
an open field a hundred yards away
two gunmen shoot women.

Yet the children still plot
with cedar waxwings,
desert tortoises,
coastal scrub sage in the lower

reaches of the coast-hugging peaks,
yellow pine and mixed
evergreens coping with
the drought conditions,
chaparral seemingly impenetrable
yet home to worlds
of animals and insects,
a wintering ground for
diving ducks,
the phases of the moon,
Mars rising at sunset.

Is this our reward or our punishment,
America the beautiful?

AMERICAN EAGLE

American eagle soars above
the crater of the old volcano,
abandoned prayers
nebulous hypocrisy clouds
morning dew apologies
scattered one by one
over the vast expanse
of privatized air and water.
Sailors in clown makeup,
apparently on
orders from the city
manager, ransacking the branch
library and an adjoining
nursery school, crashing
outboard skiffs into
the collapsing docks and
flaming taxis into
the stores, car alarms blaring
for hours set off
by the blasts. Investigators are
still trying to reconstruct
the chain of events.

The remarkable irony,
especially in view
of their bizarre reproductive
habits, is that
the general public appears
no longer even curious about it.

At the bottom of a
sunken road with high sandy
banks lined with cattails,
egrets still balance on one foot,
rusted weather cocks still spin,
minor prophets still ride swans,
erotic raccoons still wash wild ginseng,
while beneath the surface

millions of worms still chew
the earth in search of healing,
tranquility, harmony.

American eagle soars above
the crater of the old
volcano, gazing into
the caldera and dreams
of restoring the waters.

JOURNEYING TO AMERICA

In what were once
some of the city's balmiest
middle-class neighborhoods,
the withered lawns and
abandoned homes groan,
beaten and betrayed.
Recovering credible evidence in
the chaos can be difficult,
journeying to America.

But following the lockdowns,
evacuations and manhunts,
dark hearted officials
rushed to the scene where
they stopped a random
vehicle in front
of hundreds of bystanders
forced the passengers,
to their knees,
and shot them,
journeying to America.

We walked through
clumps of stonewort,
hogwort, submerged
pondweeds, lapping ripples,
a cloud of swirling flies, when
a sudden gust whipped
the still waters into
eddies and currents,
sweeping wave upon wave of
breakers hurling
coincidental debris
from the disasters
against the innocent shore.

We sought only to
preserve the knowledge

of our culture,
respect for our mothers
and grandmothers.
Deep in the crypt
of the abandoned sewer line
we drank from
a pure spring inside
an undiscovered grotto,
journeying to America.

AMERICA'S FINEST HOUR

The whirl of bats and moths
in the wizard's cave,
profound ignorance clings like a shadow
desperate salamanders glower
America's finest hour.

Officials deny the president's crimes,
martial law in Seattle
judges break out in running sores,
all night she dreams of scorpions
dour CEOs prattle
bouquets of cancer devour
America's finest hour.

A school of translucent tropical fish
dart in a different direction,
grebes build floating nests
from marsh vegetation,
the CIA denies all allegations.
The extent of the abuses
overcasts the sky with signs,
Eddie squeezes a rock
Marcia chants on the picket line,
water shut off in Baltimore
Pittsburg off limits
the guilty plead and cower
prisoners watch meteorite showers,
America's finest hour.

Goons disarmed by moms,
Truth Commission trials press on,
harbor seals lounge on the dock
stratocumulus clouds display purple,
an ant explores a petal
following round the charmed circle,
a few intertwined twigs
in the bright center of the milky way,
lovers nestled in a secret bower
America's finest hour.

AMERICA, LAND OF THE FREE

It almost seems a cosmic joke.
Unnamable terrorists
who hate all Americans
because we are the exception
in an enslaved world,
who hate us
because we are equal,
because we are free,
have declared
endless war against our freedom,
against our equality.

Right, you can't afford to get sick,
but you're created equal and free.
The awful cost of necessities
causes mothers to eat their
free and equal hearts out.
Pervasive mistrust and
seething anger rage
freely and equally through
the cities, the suburbs
and the countryside.
Skittish guards in gas masks
freely menace the
school halls piled equally
high with garbage.
Traumatized recruits with assault rifles
freely avoid the intersections,
equally wary of booby traps and
sexual transmitted diseases,
while alongside the freeway
chickens peck obliviously
at the bloated bodies
composting freely and equally
in the dust and mud of
America, Land of the Equal,
Land of the Free.

It took a woman's sense of irony
to reopen the tense confrontation,
sheering off passionate facades
of buildings, toppling overpasses, reeking
panic in crowded basements and alleys.
Swarms of officials
secretly scurried in circles frantic
to save their own skins,
unhinged for want of
an exit strategy,
while publicly
establishing calmly beyond any reasonable
doubt that their bosses the leaders of
the free world are not
connected with the desperate plots.

Thus as a last resort
to save freedom and equality
they freely and equally declared
equality and freedom
temporarily suspended indefinitely,
in an endless state of national emergency
in America, Land of the Equal
Land of the Free.

Caressed by eagle feathers
and bison hooves,
the west wind whistles through
cornflowers and yellow squash
in free fall love with
dismantled spirits,
equal blessings perfected,
nectar for the ants,
unconditional rejoicing,
rebellious wild hibiscus
freely demanding real social justice,
real freedom, real equality,
the dismantling of corporate dictatorship
in America, Land of the Equal
Land of the Free.

AMERICA'S PROMISE

I pledge allegiance to
America's promise.
I pledge defiance to
America's lie.

Defiance to
duplicity on every TV channel,
advertising campaign atrocities,
purity eaten by betrayal,
lifetimes of wilting cancer bouquets,
gallows in every school yard,
shackles on every birth certificate,
blatant fraud in every political ad,
impunity always granted,
the CEO's indictment always postponed
always the coronation of prejudice,
always the dictatorship of bread,
always the deadly fear of truth.
I pledge defiance to
America's broken promises.

I pledge allegiance to
the promises of
windswept beaches,
the openness of wildflowers,
the joy of turbulent streams
elated with their own pure power,
the passion of gentle brooks
babbling about secret loves
and heartaches,
the purity of swallows
swooping among wisps of clouds,
the perfection of snowflakes
in a child's hand,
the energy of whirligig beetles
darting among water lilies
with tubular roots buried
deep below in the rich

muck of the pond bottom.
I pledge allegiance to
the thrill of lovers' ankles intertwined,
to once-estranged sisters rejoicing
in cottonwood trees,
to rare necklaces of many-colored stones
hanging on many-colored necks of rare beauty,
to the justice of homeless prophets dancing
through abandoned warehouses,
to the healing jangle of jingle dresses
swaying at cosmic pow wows,
to the joy of social equity
among the excluded and downtrodden,
I pledge allegiance to
elders burning stock certificates,
to children overthrowing the oligarchy,
to the yet-to-be-fulfilled
American experiment,
to the revolutionary moment,
I pledge allegiance to
America's promise.

AMERICAN KNOW HOW

American know how
to rupture ancient walls with artillery shells,
mix drinking water with sewage,
descend into bloodletting
so quickly and totally that
even city workers on routine duties
are afraid to enter their own neighborhoods.
The marchers in black armbands,
the logging firms guided by deadly angels,
the owls sitting motionless almost invisible
waiting for an unsuspecting passerby,
the godfathers slitting wrists,
the wardens betraying the forests every minute.
Oily smoke spirals over
and over and over
the houses of all the children who have never
seen the sun.

Debates on the subject
at the sidewalk tables
outside the juicebar
have deteriorated into spitting contests,
while inside
our ancient family line
has exploded like a rotting watermelon.

American once knew how
to soothe a scorching tangle of emotions,
hands trembling, chest heaving,
knew how
to farm a little spread along
an oxbow cut off from
the river's course, the apparent
color a reflection of
sky or shoreline birches,
knew how
to raise generations of healthy children,
to praise spices, turtles, crystals,

to nurture fantasies of flowers
mother's milk carousels
fuschia astronomy
confessions of unending love,
the generosity of robins.
Waiting for grandfather, grandmother,
waiting for the return of
buffalos sustainers of life.
Somewhere deep inside
you can almost hear the rising murmur
of forgiveness grounded in melodies
of forgotten corners of
the inner heart of community.
American still know how,
American know how.

DEMOCRACY IN AMERICA

Ironically the gang
at the top are really just a few
punks. The time of the
oligarchs always starts like this,
unfolding in unthinkable ways
before our very eyes, with
everybody watching,
the news trickling out in spasms
reaching a crescendo when,
for example,
another five mortar rounds
kills nine, wounds forty
and mutilates the childhood of an entire
generation. Even as we speak they're
trying to destroy the evidence.
There is a continuing investigation,
of course. There always is.

Has there ever been democracy in
America? The once and future
democracy.

Perhaps it can be best understood
in the context of
of billions of years of geologic
development, during most
of which living organisms
closely resembled non-living matter.
This of course
does not necessarily
explain consciousness, intelligence,
ethics, or behavior.

No one can predict the exact moment
of the quake, but any reading of
history will tell you that,
strolling along the fault
pronghorn antelopes can hear

the schist and granite
grinding beneath. The quietest
breeze can suddenly whip into
a maelstrom, and the swiftest
stream can suddenly swirl into
a quiet pool of
democracy in America.

DISCOVERING AMERICA

Why has there been
no discovery?
Where is our collective
sense of outrage?
Are we afraid to
discover America?

Strawbosses hiding missiles in
crawlspaces, the pesticide-polluted sky
obscuring the depths of mystery,
elected officials, their strange urges
probably caused by elevated levels
of heavy metals and PCBs,
repressing the laughter of children.
Charred twisted parts of cars
and busses lie scattered nearby,
the passengers initially not knowing
whether they had been hit by
bullets or bombs or unspeakable truths.

Why is the English
language still an alien tongue
in this country,
not understood by
American wind, water,
trees or birds?

Poison festers in the wounds.
It is only because
the crimes are so great,
that they're afraid to proceed
with America's discovery.

Yet wild plants are still
edible after all these painful years.
Little twigs of
mullein stripped of bark
still have healing properties.
Ant cities still thrive

in the cracks in concrete.

Over at the abandoned capitol,
standing in the ruins
on any balmy evening,
you can almost hear
the deceit and false dreams
of self-destructing violins
still sobbing somewhere in the distance,
(this scenario replays
over and over in my head),
you can almost see
the purified spirits of cleaning ladies
dancing with their brooms
through the empty congress halls,
while the shades and shadows of millions
of ordinary people still hurl
truths like bombs
at cringing phantoms
of business-suited gangsters.

The children cry for joy
at the secrets finally revealed,
the ecstasy released,
the endurance made possible.
Now all things
suddenly overturn.
The only way forward is to
accept all historical truths
and listen to the land,
discovering America.

ONLY IN AMERICA

Forces were extorting on a maximum scale
hide indoors or get out of town
shattered glass and crumpled concrete
scattered along the sidewalk
during the interrogation
light penetration is restricted
in the day's deadliest attack
bayoneting three
workers in an ice cream shop
they only called on the soldiers to
allow food and
medicine to enter the town and
compensate the farmers for
destroying their crops while
three quarters of biodiversity
was lost
probably forever,
only in America.

Hooded youths carrying cat tails
stalked defiantly past the burning cars,
rusted missiles and corroded bombs
in the warm night rain,
met at the secret elm
and continued on,
wiring bridges and mountain tunnels
with red peonies
confessing love to carousels
sleeping in green squash and mother's milk
engulfing buildings in swans
burning sweetgrass purification
praising beaver dams and lavender bouquets
elating finger lakes
into a state of generosity
embracing the devotion of young lovers
forgiving dispirited pear trees
leading the refugees
onto the dance floor

caressing the elderly into
smooth thigh harmony
kissing imperfect souls and bodies
beyond apologies,
only in America.

THE AMERICAN EXPERIENCE

We cannot afford to wait
until they finish torching
the last corner fish market,
loot the last family bakery,
find the last midwife
sprawled dead in the corner,
cut down the last acacia tree.
Each day the prisons keep on
overflowing with a generation
of young men and women,
mostly of color,
marginalized, disenfranchised,
their only hope in crime or rebellion.
Clearly it's a case of
institutional entrapment.
But this is nothing new.
All has been going on all along,
just not being reported,
and when it was reported,
reports were meant to be
systematically ignored
in the American experience.

While our full growth
and innate possibilities
are constantly hindered
by a lack
of clean food and water,
our patrons and supervisors
turn our mutilated bodies
into decoys by the side of the road,
cautionary tales to intimidate
any following our footsteps.
When all else fails,
they pretend to
honor the fallen warriors
by awarding medals to our next of kin.
This was not the first time that

the universe became unreachable in
the American experience.

Meanwhile the winds of the four directions
continue to frame the pageant
of your great grandmother's life.
Porcupine tends the fire
of the inexorable laws of
cause and effect.
An old metal water pail ignites
your sense of wonder.
Ceremonial messengers offer
a ghost feast for the rolling hills
and timberlines lush with hawks
while blackberries offer us the power
of the rainbow.

We cannot live in the absence
of legends germinating
the seeds of rebellion and renewal.
Our aching spirits and bodies
rejuvenate as we dreams
of hardscrabble fields
suddenly bearing lush crops,
of turning injustice on its head,
of light autumn rains beginning to seep
into the dense walnut groves
of the American experience.

AMERICAN DOODLE

Back in 1776,
a *doodle* was a backcountry
bumpkin and *macaroni* were
Italian ribbons
worn on fancy hats by fashion fops.

So now almost
two hundred forty years later,
mister yokel is still riding
into town, a wild turkey tail feather
still stuck into his cockscomb,
still calling it lasagna
and still thinking himself quite the dandy.

Flaunt your bursting bombs,
toss your poison cotton candy
to all the widows weeping
around the collapsed walls
smitheened dance halls,
incinerated windows
amputated workers
shrapneled orphans
collateraled ghosts
screaming in party dresses
as thick as hasty pudding.

Don't mind the
funereal rhythms
of those tasty dirges and laments
grieving in the blowing sand,
just keep it up,
be nimble, mister doodle,
oh, that sublime noodling,
oh, rub your subprime sweaty hands
all over those abandoned girls,
stick that bloody plume
into the bullet hole in
your dented combat helmet

and call it
spaghetti, linguini,
vermicelli, fettuccini, tortellini
or whatever the fuck
you want to call it,
while the toadies
of your compliant empire
secretly pour vials of
poison into your punchbowl,
oh, blast that volume
strut that caper
jig that merry rug,
down on your jackboot heels
up on your iron toes
oh, mind that step
cut that happy beat
bust those randy moves,
be stalwart and commanding,
lift those twinkling feet,
and with all the brown-eyed girls
hiding razors in their adoring smiles,
just be handy
and everything will
be just
American Doodle Dandy.

THE AMERICAN WAY

How could something like this happen?
I don't want to judge anyone, but
only what I read in the newspapers:
the vast majority shot
execution-style, others
beaten to death, strangled, bodies
pocked with drill-holes, burns,
missing eyes, teeth, nails, limbs,
the handiwork of retired warlords and
drug smuggling bankers.
He sipped
milk slowly through
a straw to ease his ulcer,
the American way.

Metal fragments rip through
the lawn
of the traffic meridian,
erosion of public support
making politicians break out in cold sweat
and four star generals' blood boil.
Meanwhile, children give each other
their favorite toys.
In the zone between high and low tides,
among the wave-eroded rocks,
tidal pools, each a universe in itself,
and further up the dunes,
some parts of which the wind and snow
have twisted into strange shapes,
the ground bristles with
slender brushwood, a habitat
for thousands of rarely-seen creatures.
Next year this will be
a luxury hotel and golf course,
privatized by the corporations,
the American way.

Along meandering rivers

cottonwood and willows still thrive,
caterpillar tents in wild cherry trees
in the spring,
sunny openings in the canopy,
turbulence above the treeline,
a pressure-cooker environment below.
While along garden walks
and succulent terraces
the rules of engagement
strike a row of homes.
All the great works of western civilization,
written on the wings of
small nondescript brownish moths,
remain powerless to reveal
the full depths of deceit
and the full light of truth,
the American way.

IN AMERICA ON A DAY LIKE TONIGHT

On a night like today in America,
the almost-full moon
casting shadows behind us,
beating the brilliant drums
dancing through the chaparral hills.
On a day of zero visibility,
sandstorms engulfing the TV gossip columns,
overweight accountants rolling
shopping carts over concrete rubble,
comatose custodians
raising the rags upside down,
defiant frogs flipping birds,
calico cats pissing sideways
on no trespassing signs,
scarred teenagers roaming the alleys
handcuffing landlords and realtors,
scarlet tanagers hurling themselves
against barbed wire police
station windows and doors.
Neighbors pour dog
shit into stuffed ballot boxes,
while over 157,000 children
still languish in refugee camps
behind old city hall.
Meanwhile they unearth the mass graves in
the abandoned orchard, decomposing bodies
intertwined into cherry tree roots,
some still wearing socks.
In the scorched plaza the revenging angels
bleach the robes of the kneeling judges
with their own lies and impunity.
They order the F.B.I and mafia
to remove each other's
hobnailed alligator loafers.
They tie up the blindfolded bankers
with their own elastic silk garters,
line up the lawyers in size place
according to the magnitude

of their crimes.
With the harvest moon
casting brilliant shadows behind us,
we danced through the chaparral hills
beating the drums of justice,
on a day like tonight,
in America
on a night like today.

AMERICAN ROULETTE

We owe nothing to the banks
we owe nothing to the corporations
the only national debt we owe
is to the unborn generations.

Walking about the neighborhood
means courting death,
emergency rooms denying admittance to
anyone without proper papers,
which are impossible to acquire
unless of course
you have the right connections.
Into the burning pits,
entire loving families,
dumped arbitrarily along with
the smoldering husks
of looted grocery stores and restaurants.
The only items seemingly left untouched
are the parking meters and ATMs.

Spin the cylinder,
point the barrel at your head,
no regret,
don't fret,
no sweat,
everybody wins
at American roulette.

15 and a half trillion
in national debt,
they tell us,
50 thousand for
every woman, child, and man,
with 44 thousand
interest every second.

Spin the cylinder,
point the barrel at your head,
no regret,

don't fret,
no sweat,
everybody wins
at American roulette.

They tell us
we borrowed all that money
from the banks and corporations,
in order to
bail out the banks and corporations,
and pay for
the endless oil wars
waged for the benefit of
the banks and corporations.

Spin the cylinder,
point the barrel at your head,
no regret,
don't fret,
no sweat,
everybody wins
at American roulette.

Shortages of water, thought, medicine,
integrity, compassion.
Bank mercenaries deployed on roofs,
snipers arbitrarily picking off anyone who
moves too fast or too slow.
Just-enlisted deputies hurling
gasoline bombs into all the barber shops.
Municipal workers pretend to
sweep up the broken plate glass and body parts,
while in the sidewalk cafes,
constables and elected officials
still exchange makeup tips.
Suddenly ragged young girls
emerge from the alleys
throwing rocks, bottles
and honesty.

We owe nothing to the banks
we owe nothing to the corporations
the only national debt we owe
is to the unborn generations.

Or spin the cylinder,
point the barrel at your head,
no regret,
don't fret,
no sweat,
it's on the House and
the House always wins
at American roulette.

AMERICAN OVERTURN

Overturn a brand new leaf
leaf through a dog-eared book
book the d.a. for felony graft
graft a plum branch onto a peach root
root out the causes of social strife
strive toward revelatory visions
envision the end of bureaucratic dictators
dictate a hundred songs about love
love the work you live
live for wholeness and light
light the fires of forgiveness
forgive the failings of your parents
parent your children to interconnections
interconnect compassion to your world
world consciousness overturns.

Overturning privatized commons
spurning career politicians
churning ownership patents
burning corporate papers
turning over unjust laws.
Now all things American overturn.

Seamstresses unravel socks
carpenters nail their hammers
omelets flip themselves over
houses balance on their roof ridges
tree roots stretch into the air
cumulous clouds billow into back yards
senior execs pull each others' comb-overs
FBI agents bug each others' phones
peace officers club each other over the head
incumbent officeholders change their names
the president's cabinet put on false mustaches
Chamber of Commerce stuffs a brown paper bag
Secretary of the Interior hides in the closet
head of the SEC slips through the airport in drag
board chairmen arrive in the Cayman Islands

all the payoffs of all the corporate lobbyists
can't buy a jelly sandwich
citizens declare the two-party system under
arrest for impersonating democracy.

Overturning privatized commons
spurning career politicians
churning ownership patents
burning corporate papers
turning over unjust laws.
Now all things American overturn.

AMERICAN MAKE-BELIEVE

Lips meet passionate lips
in the nuanced shadows
gorgeous bodies intertwined
ecstatic dance joyful tears
soulful communion
forever whispering
infinite vows devoted depths.

Flip on the lights
giant screen torn and ragged
musty stale popcorn
rancid imitation butter
rows of empty seats
spilled soda
garbage all over the floor
smells like piss.
American make-believe.

Grammas dry their tears
with candidates' promises
scribbled on shredded ballots,
nominees all promising
home love integrity prosperity
bouquets of imaginary hot jobs
blueberry syrup avatars
on every cyber maple pancake,
belief in change and bereavement,
a young couple on a first date
pulled over by officers
in front of the high-tech playground
for reasons unclear in the report,
find their fashion-statement purse
and plastic leather wallet confiscated,
photoshopped evidence
planted in every pocket
their late-model legoland SUV hijacked
every secret digital code of decency
systematically violated

orifices stuffed with sweaty junk
and auctioned to the highest bidder
while the duly-elected mayor
restoring public order
describes the peaceful demonstration
as an organized conspiracy
of arson and looting,
but it's only American make-believe.

In the wake of three weeks of
indiscriminate bombardment
and revenge killings,
stealing fingers for souvenirs,
leaving the remnants of
the once-stately city center
in control of stylish pimps
drugged lieutenants
spitting strawbosses
TV detectives
psychotic anchormen
corrupted weathergirls flush with
sunny gusts in the 10-day forecast,
while vomit gas permeates
all the side streets
removing children's souls,
thousands wounded, unknown dead

the masked soldiers
open fire on the hospital,
the crowd scatters, hundreds trampled,
she watches her friend's leg blown off,
while not far away
they stand for hours in the freezing rain
to exercise their sacred right to vote,
but just kidding,
it's only American make-believe.

UN-AMERICAN

As un-American as these songs in the night
as the meadow jumping mouse and the red-legged frog
as the dark cloud hanging over the spot
where the pipeline burst into flames
as plant closings and layoffs
as un-American as unnamed administration sources
as the candidate pulling a fast one
as a hissing noise in the Lincoln bedroom
as unmarked graves
bureaucratic delays
toxic substances in natural foods
as barbed wire around playgrounds
as children panhandling in front of the drug store
as un-American as everywhere feelings of
helplessness, confusion, despair
as un-American as entering the mall in a camouflage vest
as afterward turning the gun on himself
as the view from Andromeda galaxy
as newlywed dandelions
as kissing under the willow tree
as damselflies swooping through bulrushes
as strings of beads of silver, turquoise, coral, shell
as the future of labor in the visions
of teenage revolutionaries
as un-American as family farm seeds
secretly handed down from generation to
generation like heirlooms
as un-American as restoring balance
as un-American as every spot on earth is sacred.

AMERICAN TRANSITIONS

transition of deputies dumping furniture on sidewalk
transition of graft in brief case to politician
transition of knife through skin
transition of finger into eye
transition from knee to groin
transition from electrode to brain
transition of cop club through skull
transition from school to bomb crater
transition from loved one to body parts

transition from submit to fight back
transition from dream to wake
transition of fist through wall
transition of rock through cop car windshield
transition of neighbors carrying furniture back into home
transition of politician to rogues gallery
transition from garbage to compost
transition from rubble to new school
transition of homeless to neighborhood
transition from resist to transform

transition from wave to shore
transition from laugh to cry
transition of winter to spring
transition from fall to fly
transition from flower to seed
transition of summer to fall
transition from wake to dream
transition from floor to wall
transition of rain to snow
transition of snow to sleet
transition from branch to sprout
transition from cook to eat
transition from sprout to leaf
transition from cloud to air
transition from seed to shoot
transition from here to there

transition from poverty to collectivity
transition from asteroid to comet
transition from isolate to socialize
transition from corporate to commons

transition from kiss to talk
transition from talk back to kiss
transition from lips to tongue
transition from tongue back to lips
transition from hips to genital
transition from genital back to hips
transition from genital to genital
transition from hips to hips

SCORCHED BIRTH

THE TRAGEDY AT THE CORE

Information on what's going on
on the ground is sketchy.
They only show us the bomber's eye view.
Reverberations of shelling bounce off
the mountain sides.
The nervous ladies chatting
about fashionable colors.
A pale thin moon circling the ring.
Misty peaks sink into the
dark surface of the bay.
Light rippling.
While the mountain passes are littered
with decomposing corpses lying
as they died.
No one approaches.
Except a bulldozer driver and six
jumpy soldiers. He dumps
dirt on top of the pile. Yet
in the midst we try
to lead decent lives, create a
just society, even love and try to
purify our human soul. Maybe
we have to just accept the
contradictions. Nearby,
a gray wolf with frightened eyes
dashes across a moonlit stream.

MUTED SHADES OF BROWN

walk along the park at night,
past the small fountain in the school yard where
women once washed clothes.
Moonlight filters through foliage
past the distant barking
of a beaten dog.
Later that night
multi-colored jasper and the essence
of trees were reduced to eating
bark and leaves,
twenty six homes were burned,
police put an automatic rifle to her cheek,
a stream of battered cars crawled
to the outskirts of town where
hundreds of drunk soldiers
blocked the road. The civic center,
an ancient market, now
no longer exists.
An old carpet, frayed along
the path to the door.
Tropical fish in deep pools in
the eyes of Emiliano Zapata.
Strange rhythms beat on clay drums.
Sky and earth become one.

THE CLOUDS' UNDERSIDES

were dark and ragged while
their tops shined and billowed
above the bare hills, almost
devoid of vegetation while
not far away, in the grass by
a whispering stream at the
very spot where wilderness
holds back civilization,
the ruins of an ancient temple
wince from shrapnel wounds.
The state of human consciousness in
our darkest age.
Vehicles scatter in charred twisted
heaps. Unsafe to go outside.
They refuse to identify the bodies.
A small girl with a redhaired rag doll,
left for dead, at nightfall crawls away.
Is this our purification by fire?

OUR LIVES ON A SUMMER BREEZE

we have nothing but our hands.
Some fifty thousand refugees
stream out, the report states,
independently confirmed.
Rocket-propelled grenades punch
holes in all the barn roofs,
looting rampages along main street,
no food or medicine getting through,
she picks up the baby,
cluster bomb explodes,
you prick yourself on a thorn:
your lover is lying to you
one drop of blood sits on your fingertip.
a huge antlered stag silhouettes for an instant
against the night sky.
Rebuilding shattered dreams.

THE SUN ROSE ON A FOGGY

rain-soaked rags in the gutter
chalk drawings of disturbed children
living in abandoned houses
blackened roof shingles scattered across
floors inlaid with precious stone
piles of broken toys sinking
into moist earth at the bottom of the pit
charred dismembered dreams lying where they died
mass graves strewn with
rotting hearts and burnt minds
roof beams lying across the kitchen table
their village still off limits
until its goals are achieved
the ten American corporations
which own the media
ordered them to leave or be shot
when she realized that she had to live bravely
and the sun shines darkness too

SHEET METAL FLAPS IN THE BREEZE

jets strafe the country road
packed with the day's refugees
fireballs over the vegetable market
a premature greenness haunts the fields
blind men wash the streets
magpies wing above the ruins
sprouts still encircle the stump
the eldest would have been eight years old
she haunted recesses of his mind
all those wasted years

nothing at the scene evidenced
a military target.

ALL OF OUR MEN ARE GONE

a rain of frogs
broken pitcher
the point at which hope is extinguished
muffled explosions echo from the mountain sides
a cousin shot dead
he thinks they are in hiding
endless chorus of loss
nestled in the folds of the valley
the old thatched roof
lumps of black earth in plowed fields
a clean bare room
walking along the empty shore
an early spring rain
girl who dreams great dreams.

VEIL OF MIST AROUND THE SUN

movement of light through the leaves
her glove in his hand
the pool surrounded by willows, lilacs, gladioli, irises
city burning for the fifty-fifth day
tourists replaced by terrorists
launching a major new offensive
the vast majority out all night in rain
impossible to confirm casualty figures
as air raid sirens sounded again at mid-morning
along with his two sons
intelligence on the ground is sketchy
she has the look of a madwoman
a starry night with cypresses
I wish you could fill your lungs with it

A FEW OLD MEN HAVE FOUND SHELTER IN THE BASEMENT

What kind of love did I feel
ten days hiding in the woods
smoldering tractors and trailers
spinal fractures, every degree burns
allowed to return to the rubble of my home
the roof of the freight depot scattered on the sidewalk
many crows circling about
the trail along the inlet from the sea
street lamps reflected in puddles
view from the school window
woman beside a cradle
an abundant growth of green moss

TOWERS SILHOUETTE AGAINST THE SKY

towers silhouette against the sky
opening the prison
of a three-headed bird
wiring bridges and mountain tunnels with explosives
a wedding party in front of the door
a small demon with an insect body
his face, peacefully radiant, remote from his torturers
the acrid smell of smoke filling the streets
hide indoors or get out of town
many arrived shaking and in tears
the top floors had collapsed
an ancient woman sweeping away the glass and debris
the shrub-covered hills at dusk, the evening star rising

FALLING FROM THE CLOUDS

Falling from the clouds like a swarm of insects
forces were extorting on a maximum scale
his body a broken egg shell
sitting alone at the bay window
sad red roofs with smoking chimneys
a mass of refugees mulling along
near the chemical factories
stray missile hits a large white drawbridge
under which a barge passes
an old man at the tiller
autumn trees in spring

A ROW OF HILLS

a row of hills, blue in the evening mist
a few geese pecking at grass
a woman, hands calloused from hard work,
bends and picks up
a huge fire raging at the hospital
a deep crater blown out of one corner
a stray bomb between a school and a farmhouse
plunging down from the roof to the first floor
as firetrucks converged on
the smoking residential district
damaging railways and watermelons
water mains shooting like geysers
a small globe of earth placed carefully
upside down on a gallows
devoured by birds
flashes of catastrophes at sea
poisoned by the magician's wand
we seem to be imprisoned in some cage
these bleak winter days
lilac hues in the evening sky
like a field of young tomatoes, inexpressibly pure
dew appears in the grass
a sow with a litter of sucklings
in the twilight of that deep shadowy elm
how much light there is in darkness!

IN EARLIER ATTACKS

in earlier attacks yesterday
a flame shot out of a swan's beak
the expression of a sleeping baby
took refuge in a hole in the wall
thick black smoke filled the streets
closer to madness than to childhood
some bleeding from shrapnel wounds and others
from the glazed look of exhaustion
firefighters trapped inside
the weight of a fabric
while an old fool, fascinated by
the tricks of the illusionist,
does not see the blue demon
next to him playing a clarinet

VIEW FROM THE BARRED WINDOW

1

the clouds stayed red long after the sun had set
over the massive explosions at the dental clinic,
injuring at least twenty seven memories
of plants and crustaceans like gnarled
trees with fantastic roots, while
the vast majority spent the night
in the rain, huddled along the road
cutting through fields of young green corn

2

the entire side wall was blown away, leaving
the TV studio with its two top floors
collapsed, a charred ruin, while an owl sat
on the withered branch of a hollow tree and
watched the river, as calm as a pond,
reflecting light of the gibbous moon

3

sunset behind clouds
the dreamer tripped over the long shadows
and fell into a well while the tide was
out, the water very low, but twisted hawthorn
bushes, their branches bent low to one
side by the wind, hampered rescue efforts, so
the doctors amputated his sense of compassion
to free him

4

chunks of concrete and broken glass
scatter over the ground; on the

horizon a strip of light, above it immense
dark clouds and slanting streaks of rain;
many trees lie about uprooted; a man
leans against the bridge rail, looks into
the dark water; birds begin to
sing at the first hint of dawn

THE RAVEN SPOKE ABOUT THE WAR
under conditions of anonymity

1

white-crested waves as far as the eye can see
killed by paramilitaries
writers and schoolteachers, executed yesterday,
shed a golden light over the fields
a red brick house covered in ivy
blames the flight of wild ducks
while an elderly walled garden
blooming with lilacs and dogwood
exhausted, in a state of shock,
sleeps in doorways and on sidewalks

2

babbling brooks are caressed by
the spiral of violence
air raid sirens sound confessions of love
smooth thighs praise grim pictures
children stare out of windows, solemn and gloomy,
egrets charbroiled beyond recognition
food medical supplies glide over pools of mother's milk
anti-aircraft missile kissed beyond exhilaration
bodies of foxes crash into forgiveness

3

first robin of spring balancing funerals
lawyers pound earthworms for a sixth day
extremist groups rejoice under cottonwood trees
spreading sweet nothings like propaganda on the dance floor
pearl necklaces surround thousand of refugees
as terrorists hurl passionate melodies on violins
engulfing the buildings in a balmy afternoon

4

sparrows whisper about the troubled province
hydrangea shake the city with strong intimations
red peonies hit by surface-to-air missiles
carousels executed on Sunday
fantasies of crystal shot dead by police
ethnic hatred snapped the turtle's endurance
gas masks dumped into corn flowers
reliable sources reported

5

pounding the southern city with strange haunting pictures
featherless birds launch new attacks against targets
dozens of missiles strike the tree shaped like a hand
as a parade of naked men seated on animals of every kind
fire missiles at three-fifteen a.m.
on the populated part of the city
helicopters and snipers augment the usual security forces
with laws of color, unutterably beautiful
while a grove of olive trees, dark against the glimmering sky
announces it is sending additional troops
and jets pummel a broad swath
across the disturbing tranquility of a woman

FIELDS OF CINNABAR

BEADED CURTAINS

you peek through the beaded curtains
and see the moon gliding through a thin cloud;
you and your lover lie scarcely moving
for a long long time while a brook
trickles through your hearts.
suddenly the straw boss is handing you
your paycheck five dollars short,
you lean your boot heel into the shovel
and look up into the snowflakes.
they try to break through
the picket line but a bleeding sunset
fills the entire sky

TAKING CARE OF BUSINESS

an exploitation of human labor business
a looking out for number one business
a make your pile and get out business
a boss order abomination business
a whatever the market will bear business
a cheat lie steal business
a do what you're told or else business
a degradation inflation depression toxic wastes business
a hemorrhoids beat your best friend business
a draft plutonium gangster business
an atomic dust imperial world war three business
a business as usual business

where is the honesty of penguins?
where is the justice of sunrise?
must free people be prepared to sleep as well
in garages, under bushes or in dreams?
even at this moment the boardmembers meet
in the condemned sewer to divide our livers
into exacting shares, sealing the fate
of munition profits on
our ability to have children

a rapture stars tumble along your spine business
a fields of orange poppies spread their knees to the mountains
of your eyes business
a mass demonstration rubbed with alchemical smoke business
a conch shells withdrawing energy from stuffed ballot boxes
business
a lifting the consecrated picket line to the east business
a boycott all businesses business
a submachineguns melt in cops screaming hands business
a collectivizing your boss' business business
an abolishing business
a taking care of business

CHILDLIKE INNOCENCE ALWAYS

corruption injustice abuse
captivity injury anguish
Choking inhuman abasement
Chile Indonesia Angola
cobwebs insanity ambush
conspire intruder assassin
cobra infernal agony
Chad Iraq Argentina
cartridges impale assault
cannibal internment autopsy
cancer intimidate aghast
coup intervene asphyxiate
Cuba India Algeria
Cambodia Ireland Arabia
colonial incorporated aggression

challenge insurgent accusing
companions invoke agitation
courage illumine awaken
confiscate imagine abolish
collective indigenous alliance
commune international augury
cleansing infinite acquittal
climax intimate absolution
compassion insight amnesty
childlike innocence always
C.I.A.

WAR ARTIST

war artist, trained in trauma school
rehearsed to act a bloody part
and now so downhearted
cause we ain't letting you practice your art

the general wakes with a sour stomach
the general examines his toilet paper for blood
the general is upset at the state of his jelly and toast
the general calls for his metallic wraparound sunglasses
the general decides to alter the statistics
the general bumps into his wife's lover at the urinal
the general's doctor's late for the day's first injection
the general orders the sailor to strap on the dildo and fetch the whip
the general steps into the conference room and strides confidently up to the pinned map

war artist, strutting there
with your neutron bombs corseting your flabby sections
you're going to find someday
you can't hide from your shadow and your reflection
you can't hide from your shadows and your reflections

CREATES

creates the Indian Ocean
blows a silver ring around the moon
runs his tongue along his lover's burning ridge
tears up ballot in front of voting booth
rides the wave of the marching chant
constipates the chairman of the board
heals a bleeding mind
kisses a pimple on her lover's ass
thanks a sparrow for a song
takes a bite from the cat's dish
ties the ideologist's shoelaces together
abolishes the credit card
radiates in waves of pleasure through your lover's dream body
knocks over the daffodils, exposing the hidden
microphone to the general strike committee
loosens your pelvic shores
shares his carrot with his little brother
denies the charges
disappears down a drain pipe
trisects the pentagon
gives the broker three years parole
reveals Dick Chaney's novocaine habit
pulls off Newt Gingrich's buttons
appears as a great dane at four a.m. in Bush's bedroom
takes a long piss on the J. Edgar Hoover memorial blackjack
steps into Ronald Reagan's dream dressed like
Mother Jones with her sleeves rolled up
throws a family reunion
soaks all the beans overnight in a big pot
hands out the bowls and spoons
passes round the fair shares
creates

WITH THE PROLIFERATION
(of advanced weaponry, nuclear war becomes an increasing statistical probability)

you squat by a log fire
a sunshower passing a country road
your thigh muscle stretches to Borneo
the tiny soft hairs on the hill of your buttock
a salamander sits beneath a cherry tree
your sweetheart in overalls
each leaf forms around its energy absorbers
the secret meaning in that look in your eye
a house remembers all of its visitors
shavings twist off a pencil into negative space
a bluebell is heartsick for a false lover
logs jamming galactic river
being weighed down by "the lessons of history"
I had a good boss once: he kept apologizing
they better not try to close that window before
we get our food stamps
a train wheel crushes a grasshopper
brigades of landlords landmine the trail to the source
a scarlet tanager contemplates suicide
stop I've seen enough

evening breezes fill the heads of state
oppression breeds the struggle against itself
a green marble rolls down a stone path
a sudden storm drenches a financier
worm breaking in half
river of honey flows through a thirsty cavern
your sweetheart taking off overalls
spinning on the edge of the world
a picketline encircles the great silence
you notice a universe in the palm of your hand
following your heart through a concrete wall
you see god leaping in the embers

spell to prevent the next world war
a million grandmothers surround the pentagon

the president is attacked by a poem in the getaway car
I heard it on the unemployment line
missiles misfire on launching pads
the neighbors march on city hall
unpiling the money of the world
becoming all you know you can be
history means nothing unless
you're willing to risk everything for love
always expect the impossible

THE DESTATUIZATION OF LIBERTY

the executive calls the senator at the monopoly hernia
money bunion castration too much perfume
mass picketing is declared illegal
insurance abomination swallow your tongue
your lover's hand is like dry ice
a pillar of salt looks back at Gomorrah

liberty mourns through the dirty barred window
meets her lover in a secret melody
liberty roaming through the night forest
in purifying agony

you run your tongue along your lover's ocean cheek
you will be neither employer nor employee
the chairman of the board is paraded through the jeering streets
Paine and Jefferson go on a great wandering
collectivization is circulation of light
why did the lovers sleep with their glasses on?
the better to see their dreams

YOUR LOVER'S NECK

you touch your lover's neck
beneath a willow heavy with wind;
crystals slide into each other but
the cop's hand is grasping your shoulder;
they drag you into the interrogation room
when at the galactic center
your sweetheart slips into something
a little more comfortable,
you are inspired by the skin
of an apricot and escape together
on a winged deer through the forest

BETWEEN

mud oozes between your toes
you notice a twig catch
on a mossy rock in a backwhisper
of the current as your landlord's face
appears in the drenching rain,
you grasp for the fire opal but
it vanishes, all prisoners for
crimes against property are released,
a green-tailed bird alights on your lover
in bed you pull down the covers and climb
along the edge of tomorrow
into a grove of ferns

CONSCIOUSNESS OF

the way you unhook your brassiere
running barefoot through a country puddle
a calico cat in a deepest yawn
what we are and what we can be
a bird of paradise outside your window
being forced to take a factory job
the moment you first realized America is not very democratic
the root system of every plant you see
being careful not to step on a black beetle
the surgeon sutures the incision
your lover whispers in your ear
the thoughts of the ocean at sunset
a puma climbs a cherry tree
allying the nations of our mind
into a new resurgence deep
in an awesome future
we walk beyond dreamless sleep.

THREE QUICK JABS

1

Dick Chaney, ordering out the national guard,
bites his tongue in the same spot twice,
while a log drifts in the middle of the ocean
and a great bird appears in the evening sky

2

as the general strike moves
into its third day, the bombardiers
are put on ready alert, the vomitgas
canisters are discovered defective,
the Secretary of War keeps appearing at the toilet door,
a bee climbs into a chrysanthemum

3

sunset flashes off a mountain top,
the brigadier breaks and runs,
a cat peeking out of a brown paper bag,
the lover is awakened by a sweet hand,
Bush dictating his confession,
a young hummingbird stretches her wings,
the stocks are fed into the shredder,
a raindrop on the back of your hand

OF TWO EVILS

Mussolini spits at Hitler (behind his back)
peace candidate Quasimoto bombs the restless ghost of LBJ
Jimmy Carter the Lesser sticks his little finger in Bush's left ear
Ronald Reagan the Greater sucks the petroleum products
out of Richard Nixon's steering gear

let the slavedriver hire the judge
let the vice president's plot be hatched
let the party hacks dream of blood
let the vice squad's ravaging disease
your lover slips a hand inside your shirt
the scent of lilacs rustles the leaves
I'd go to Budapest to spend a night with you
your kiss your lover's secret desire

children crayon the senate
an act of god illumines this very moment
your former boss asks permission to take a break
the money belongs to the hungry
democracy is evicting your landlord
the two party system means we're not invited
party collectivist it's always election day
vote in the streets
rock me all night long

BE A UNION ORGANIZER

union disunion reunion communion unison unity
labor union trade union industrial union
union card union hall union meeting union songs
union shop union label union benefits union
hacks union dues union pension fund union racketeers
break the union company union business unionism union
history union struggles one big union revolutionary
unionism union of workers union of industries union
of like minds union of black and white union of women
and men union of soul and heart union of elders and
children union of sensual and spiritual union of lowest
and highest union of winter and summer union of
red and green union of earth and sun union
of shore and tide union of muscle and energy stream
union of seeker and sought union of something and nothing
union of birth and death union of profundity and
absurdity union of sperm and egg union of freedom
and necessity union of socialism and democracy union
of form and meaning union of laughter and
tears union of communities and nations
union disunion reunion communion unison unity
BE A UNION ORGANIZER

SUNRISE AND SUNSET

sunrise and sunset last all day long
a lover's thigh is kissed in a field of clover
strings of pelicans glide above the breakers
as we run hand in hand along the tide
your sweetheart awakes with a ruby in his mouth
the sounds of rainforest echo in your soul
I melt when you say that to me
they order the bombs into production
another hungry welfare cheat is caught
worker replaced by machine
the executioner licks his teeth
someone reads the marriage of heaven
and hell in the street
a baby is sobbing in a desolate gutter
the archbishop appears at the tattoo parlor
a gaggle of politicians try to hang themselves
the presses jam against lies so there are no newspapers
the stockbrokers and hypocrites blaming each other
the computers all spit the same answer
ninety-four senators testify they've lost their memory

the day the world was saved

all the conflicting ideologies announce it proves them right
a Harris poll shows 23% opposed
the orangutans were busy fucking
a little girl asked her older sister, what does saved mean?
I've loved you secretly for a long time

AN ALPHABET OF U.S. CORPORATIONS WITH INVESTMENTS IN EL SALVADOR

Alcoa Aluminum
Bristol-Myers
Crown-Zellerbach
Dow Chemicals
Exxon
Foremost Dairies
General Motors
Hanover Insurance
IBM
Jack Off A Dead Pig
Kimberly-Clark
Lynching The Spirit Of Jaguars
Max Factor
Nestle
Otis Elevator
Pan Am
Quagmire Beneath Your Feet
Ralston Purina
Sears Roebuck
Texaco
Underwood Meats
Vea La Luna Muerta
Warships Cruise Off The North Shore
Xerox
Yelling Disembowelment
Zigzag Lightning Splits The Stock
Yet The Children Cannot Be Destroyed
X-Out The Name On The Deed
Why Are You Doing This To Your Sister
Violar La Tomba De Los Loros
Undressed By The General's Bloodthirst
Tronchando El Three M Company
Standard Oil Explodes On Saturday
Rocks Tumble Down A Narrow Gorge
Quaking The Treasurer's Beachhouse
Proctor And Gamble Palido Como Copos De Jabon
Orden Spits Poison Writhing On Its Side

Never Push The People Too Far
Mutilando Monsato Chemical Dividendos
Liars Shuddering Like Wet Vultures
Kneecap Splatter On The Steps Of The Capital
Judgment In Long Shadows
IT&T Being Hereby Served Notice
Hearing Jugular Unions De Aranas Y Angeles
Gunbarrel In The General's Soft Corporation
Folgers Coffee Bankrupted by Armed Grandmothers
Entering Illuminated Territory
Duendes Surface On The Assembly Line
Cleansing Chevron Oil From The Common Plantation
Banco De América Surrounded By Visionaries
América Central Oceanic Amazement

THE COMMISSAR

the commissar orders you to step behind the line
the government owns the industries so it's illegal to strike
the chairman-for-life strides to the podium
to thunderous applause and announces
the central committee's unanimous decision
in the interest of the working people

social justice is / social justice is not
you scrub your sweetheart's back
helping your neighbor fix a window
reading a story to a sick child
a blackberry flower opens its soul to the wind
hold hands at the movies
dip your spoon into the honeypot
pass beyond the verbal mind
loving with your soul
defy authority
abolish all bossism
take your fair share no less no more
squatting on the earth, stretching to the sky

PAINTING A TIGER

painting a tiger in realistic detail
then reaching in and pulling its tail
we must be visible down through the marrow

midwives of transitions
the language of dream
the hinges of realities

composting the same conscious ground

before the act
during the act
after the act:
the WORD

you know you got it if it moves you

FORMATION OF THE NEW INTERNATIONAL

a chainsaw breaks the silence
Hitler commits suicide
decadence is a scarce commodity better grab your share
man I'd like to get into her pants
the moment after you die
and what of the voice in the embers
I know you have visions too
hey we got a common ancestor
lifting the spirit from the cell
you blow at a house of draft cards
Rockefeller dives into an oil slick
the reactor is unveiled at the wax museum
singing from your higher self
a honeysuckle stretches into a pecan tree
the sound of waves on a moonless night
sweetcrotch on a Sunday morning
socialism makes us feel good
only we can save ourselves.

O COLUMBIA

O COLUMBIA

O Columbia
this is the temple
these endless waves of trees
this wolfbirch dawn
these rivers of light bursting through crevices of cloud
this sweet fogdamp wombsky
this starry flight of geese
this is the temple
this forestdrenched sunset
this symphony of clover
these antelope mesas rainrumbling
these snowloving islands
this threethousandmile bouquet of grainflowers returning to
seedwarmth
this moondamp redwood knowledge
this thrushmelody shimmering through this golden spine
this marriage of root and earth
this revealing of oceangreen valleysecrets
these clustered mountaintops singing to the dawn
this holy gift of rabbit leaf and wind
this joyous drifting continent
this is the temple

But the moneychangers have seized the temple
this cancer salesman
this tv news disguise
this shattered glass betrayal
this genocide of falcons
this prison corporation factory torture
this wageslave firing squad
this starvation graft insurance noose
this money infection
this poisoned barbedwire bank
this groaning captivity
this gangster orgy
this chairmen of the board conspiracy
this wagecut vice president heartattack
this stockholder deathship speedup

these neutron War Secretary embalmings
this incorporated lobotomy
these brokenhearted bleedingroots
this crucifixion of robins
this burning lake this storm of nails

the moneychangers have seized the temple

O these selfevident truths
O these alienated rights
O this consciousness streaming
O this vast comingtogether
O this great castingout
O this refusal to obey orders
O this national strike
O this army rebellion
O this wilderness insurrection
O these marching saints
O this deep plowing
O this whip of cords
O this drivingout of the moneychangers
O this dissolving of the corporations
O this cleansing of the temple
O this tearingoff of uniforms
O this bomb dismantling
O this fence downtearing
O this prison unlocking
O this mind unblinding
O this hurtlover healing
O this return to foreststars
O this rebirth of our crystalhearts
O this sunburst of workerlove
O this seagull marriage
O this rebuilding of the temple
O this collective jewel
O this thought of love among us
O this emerald thunder
O this tongue on your perfect lips
O this raven's shout
O this festival of our ancestors

O this ceremony of dawnfamily
O this communal money
O this collective land
O these socialized machines
O this economic democracy
O this joyful workers' power
O this rainbow cooperation
O this circle of love around us
O these laughing children
O these joined genitals shining
O this infinite sharing
O this living prophesy
O this dance of liberation
O these hugs among the cultures
O this love among the races
O this harmony of light
O this kiss blown from the sun to the moon
O this ocean of hearts
O COLUMBIA

LONG AGO

Long ago, the old ones say,
the earth was common garden to us all:
the trees dropped us
fruit to share, sweet leaves
stems and flowers offered themselves up
to all of us
through the endlessly living soil,
from above and below the branches and rocks
gifted us common tools, we taught
each other how to fish and cook,
hunt and sew, shared abundance when
the earth glowed warm, shared
our stores and body heat
when we huddled together from ice and storm;
so together we tended the garden.

But today I drive my old beatup wheels
up and down the garden's rows and
everywhere above the clatter and drone
of crazy machines
I can hear the cast-out people's
wail and moan, the same rumbling
down every foodstamp and unemployment line,
the same sulking anger in so many
eyes along the street,
and the schools seethe like
concentration camps, the workplaces reek
of war, at so many kitchen tables
the same cries burst through grit teeth,
and everywhere is electric fence and barbed
wire, security guards, burglar alarms,
keep out, private property, trespassers
will be violated to the fullest strong
arm of the law . . .

THIS IS NOT DEMOCRACY
THIS IS DICTATORSHIP

down with the dictatorship
of money and property
down with the dictatorship
behind paper walls
down with the dictatorship
of the corporations

DISSOLVE THE CORPORATIONS

REBIRTH TO THE GARDEN
AS COMMON BIRTHRIGHT OF US ALL

MIXED BREEDS

His mother has some Italian blood in her
her lover's just a bit Hungarian Jew
his grandpa's got some Chicano in him too
her aunt's one part Madagascan
his cousin's a little Choctaw
neither you nor he know it but
there's some Malay-Swede in your uncle-in-law

Mixed breeds
that's what we all really are
no fences ever succeeded
in keeping our loveplasm apart:
we were one in the beginning
and the tribes have traveled far
but we're reaching home again
and we've the right to claim what's ours:
our blood is an ocean
flowing round and round the world:
the future belongs
to the mixed breed and proud

THANK YOU GRANDMOTHER
(For The People of Tó Hajiiléého)

The desert throbs and rumbles.
Painted horses on the scrub piñon mesas
sniff the bristling wind and rear.
Diné, The People,
gather from the mountains of the four directions
for a great singing
swelling like sunrise over the medicine
and spreading with the fireglow
over the blowing night sands.

Behind the front seats of the pickups
parked in a haphazard circle in the dunes,
bluish rifle barrels glimmer.

Grandfather strolls along the parched arroyo bank,
arms clasped behind his back.
Noticing a smooth flat pebble,
brown with gray streaks pointing east,
he stoops and picks it up.
Turning it over he sees a rainbow:
Grandfather smiles.

Grandfather,
with a trail of deputies' clubs hanging high over your head
come to us groaning
with hunger on the ends of your wings
come to us writhing
in old age sleeping in gutters
come to us bleeding
with barbed wire streaming from your bruises
come to us moaning
in your rags wove from cornstalks
come to us screaming
wandering along the plutonium scars of stolen land
come to us crashing
eating out of garbage cans holy with buckskin
come to us tearing

with school lies tattooed on your shoulders
come to us sobbing
cheated at the store in your thirst of white bean stalks
come to us pleading
with thunder sweating from your eyes
come to us throbbing
from your doorway of sand and cloud-darkness
come to us crowing
with the mirages of youth tied about your feet with white lightning
come to us breathing
kissed by the winds of dark mist and pollen
come to us shining
from your porch of squash blossoms
come to us laughing
rubbed with the breath of dawn
come to us glowing
in your coat of children and rivers
come to us roaring
with a trail of dew draping over your shoulders
come to us cleansing
drenched with the stomachs of mountains
come to us singing
in freedom running along the streams of evening twilight
come to us flashing
licked with the shirts of our ancestors
come to us flooding
with deer playing in your shadow
come to us filling
rolling in a robe of comets
come to us dancing
with your rifle loaded with sunrise
come to us shooting
with eagle leaping from your eyes
come to us Grandfather
come to us Grandfather

Ahéhee nihiMásání, ahéhee nihiMásání
Thank you Grandmother, thank you Grandmother

STRICTLY CONSTITUTIONAL

Went to a party on the courthouse stairs:
you should have heard that bad band wail:
the sax was smoking down the drummer's tail
while the guitar melted the locks on the jail

the night the dockets caught fire
and we boogied from darkness to dawn
you should have been there with us carrying on
the night the stocks caught fire

Harry said to Mary, "Look here comes the heat
better stash your stash and get your shoes on your feet"
Mary said to Harry, "Lover don't be dismayed
it's only the comrades from the Emma Goldman Brigade"

the night the dockets caught fire

Firetrucks arrived like a flock of screech owls
but they just couldn't breech our surging wall
when we locked arms and howled,
you should have seen the chief,
his face hanging like a side of beef
and his eyes rolling wild, crying,
"Think about the governor, consider the neighbors"
as we carried out the deeds, the police files
and the incorporation papers

the night the stocks caught fire

Hooting and stomping like unchained slaves
round those prancing embers and those sky-licking flames
when the music suddenly stopped and we turned and saw
a shadow standing by the courthouse door,
draped in a hood and long black robe,
yelling, "Stop in the Name of the Holy Ghost!"

But Ghost,
who was leaning against a broken lamp post,
just laughed, fingered His Holy Nose

and went right back to His Marshmallow Roast

the night the dockets caught fire
and we boogied from darkness to dawn
you should have been there with us carrying on
the night the stocks caught fire

A pale moon still hovered in the west
the east was singed with dawn
we hung upon each others' necks
swaying back and forth
a pigeon settled on the flagpole mast
the band jammed slow
thin smoke swirled through the waking streets
ashes started to blow

TWO STREET SHOUTS

1
Capitalism tears the family of races apart
but fighting back together can heal our aching heart

2
Social revolution means shedding diseased skin
and mending the circle whole again

WHEN I ENTERED THIS HOUSE

When I entered this house
they told me, "There's opportunity here for all.
You'll make it, kid, if you work hard
& you keep something on the ball."

But since then I've wandered
up & down the dim-lit stairs
& met philosophers pushing brooms
& nincompoops swiveling in university chairs,

& since then I've peeked in their secret rooms
& glimpsed how they *really* run this thing.
I just want to warn you, kid,
in this house the toughest crook is king.

DOLLARS

I looked at a dollar
bill the other day and
noticed to my surprise there
is no dollar sign on the dollar
A spread
eagle, a wide
eye floating over
a pyramid, George
Wash in a curly wig, a burnt
forest of ones but
no dollar sign.
then I realized
it wasn't so strange
afterall there are no
dollarsigns on bombers' wings either,
on the sides of
nuclearplants or in incense-
shrouded shrines in
banks

ROCKEFELLER'S DEAD

remember his great grandpa drew his first blood money selling
cancer cures in the 1830s
rockefeller's dead
remember his grandpa invented the game of all's fair in war and
monopoly in the 1870s
rockefeller's dead
remember his father ordered a tent city of striking miner
families shot and burned at Ludlow Colorado in 1914
rockefeller's dead
remember the body piles at Attica prison in '71 remember the
Vietnam war remember Nixon remember the
MafiaNeutronBombColdWarJoeMcCarthyRonaldReaganGasCh
amberBankVault
ROCKEFELLER LIVES
remember Standard Oil Chase Manhattan Bank IBM Mobil
CBS Borden Atlantic-Richfield AT&T Metropolitan Life Allied
Chemical Con-Edison Chemical Bank Eastern Airlines Pan-Am
American Express etcetera etcetera
remember the next time cops attack strikers the next time
somebody's sentenced to jail for stealing what's rightfully theirs
remember the next imperialist war remember the crime family
that still chairs the juntaboard
ROCKEFELLER LIVES
remember there has always been and will always be a
RESISTANCE

I DREAMED I SAW MY PICTURE IN THE POST OFFICE

W-A-N-T-E-D
for jaywalking parking in noparking zones
cutting labels off pillows of stuffed chairs
littering driving stoned slipping personal notes into fourthclass mail
charging longdistance credit card calls to board of directors' phones
running out on bank loans
shoplifting apples paper clips and underwear
scraping a Ferrari and splitting the scene
tax and draft evasion
harboring a deserter from the marines
lying on federal applications
punching coinchanging machines
slipping past Welfare regulations
sawing down highway advertising billboards with a bow saw
conspiring with known revolutionary agitators and outlaws

and for using foul and abusive language to officers of the peace

IF YOU HAVE INFO LEADING TO THE WHERE
CALL YOUR LOCAL SECRETPOLICE

CAUTION:
OTHERS MAY BE WITH HIM
THEY MAY BE ARMED TO THE TEETH
(upon seeing my picture in the Post Office rack, as you can surmise, I was taken aback. Then sensing the serious of my situation without further hesitation slipped toward the door before I might be recognized. But the clerk at the Stamp Window was staring at me. I panicked and was about to flee when I realized that he and the other clerks and people standing in line...
...all looked exactly like me

FACES

Who gets to sleep in a windblown hovel
guts aching with hunger
and who gets to jet from sun-quenched beach
to alpine ski lodge on a caprice?

this is a face of dictatorship

Last month the landlord raised our rent
we refused to pay
sent us a notice
vacate in three days
time was up
came back with his police
threw everything we owned
out into the street

this is a face of dictatorship

Spokesmen sing, There isn't enough to go round.
While rats grow sleek on hoarded corn
and silk-suited farmmasters
order milk poured into the ground

this is a face of dictatorship

Injunction said, two pickets at each entrance
was all we strikers could have
but twice a day the bulls cruised round
to run protection for the scabs

this is a face of dictatorship

Jetplane up there
ripping my clouds, splattering my air,
are you pregnant with grain to balm away despair
or bombs to seed the soil somewhere?

this is a face of dictatorship

Bluejeans and business suit fighting in the street

red lights howl sirens chilling sweep
nightsticks flash hungry for meat
which head is going to get beat
bluejeans or business suit?

this is a face of dictatorship

This classroom teaches American democracy:
do what you're told
sit in your seat

this is a face of dictatorship

Faces of dictatorship:
the banker's pen, the boss' knife,
the politician's smile,
you've been seeing them all your life:
we've had to fight them to survive
since before we knew who or how

DEFACE THE DICTATORSHIP
Don't give up now

LA COMMUNE, PARIS 1871

and yet today in the USA they let us all survive
only cause we each got a good disguise

Well,
all I know is
I am still now and here,
still looking through these hundred billion windows
at my self over there.

I cried when I heard the war was over and
when I remember
the war still rages on,
I cry again and once again recall

I am a warrior
and gird my trembling loins like
Arjuna,
and dare to breathe the holy air,
sharpen these songs,
prepare this creaking flesh.

To resolve my pain I
must resolve yours, and
that is why
we must risk and risk again,
and recall that beneath our clothes
we are still as naked as when we were born,
and underneath it all
we are still communards.

FOR THE INNOCENTS

all who have ever heard the message of the crickets
we call on you
all who have ever felt the wind splashing cleanly in your face
we call on you
all who have ever loved someone of another race
we call on you
all who are, or are descendants of
wageslaves serfs slaves prisoners debtors tenants housewives foreigners
we call on you
all who believe in the inalienable human right of the oppressed
to throw off their oppressions and oppressors
we call on you

the night of the shame beyond madness is upon us
the despisers of sunrise
musicians of the ghastly dance
sorcerers grislier than hollywood movies

the night of those whose unquenchable destruction gushes from rivers of self-hate
whose murderous passions warp from the slaughtered children inside themselves

Even as these innocents are cowardly murdered one by one on city streets,
their elder brothers' deaths thousands by thousands on faroff colonial shores
are being brazenly plotted in conference rooms,
their families' destruction millions by millions in wageslave pauperdom
is being flauntingly conspired
in those same plush chairs

I call down the spirit of Harriet Tubman and Angelina Grimke
the voice of Frederick Douglass and William Lloyd Garrison
the wrath of Nat Turner and Elizabeth Gurley Flynn
the heart of Sojourner Truth and Martin Irons
the strength of Thomas Paine and W.E.B. DeBois

the balance of Martin Luther King and Mother Jones

race war . . imperialist war . . . class war . . .
what's it all for . . ?

all who have ever heard the message of the crickets
we call on you
listen to the evidence

all who have ever felt the wind splashing cleanly in your face
we call on you
pass sentence

all who have ever wept at the mercy of spring
we call on you
stand with folded arms as a surrounding wall and carry out the sentence

for the innocents.

WHO RULES AMERICA?

Who rules America?
you and me?
Those goodol'boys they parade on tv?
Or faceless shadowed faces
hiding behind incorporation papers un-
listened telephones and stainless steel secretaries,
meeting the board behind locked doors
and directing our lives invisibly?

Is the twopartysystem democratic and free?
or are those candidate-
selections really
a masquerade in a smokescreen?
Setups between feuding gangs inside
ONEBIGMONEYPARTY
in a never ending brawl
over how to split the booty?

Who rules America?
you and me?
Lord, it's hard
to fight an enemy it's hard to see

A NIGHT AT THE CIRCUS

Headline of Souvenir Program:
RECESSION OVER PRESIDENT DECLARES
And everybody in the tent can smell bad breath
yeah, MONOPOLISTS RIDING HIGH
While we smolder on unemployment lines,
patch threadbare clothes,
watch our bankbooks stamped CLOSED,
can't afford to go anywhere or turn on the lights,
open the refrigerator all you see is white
and even the alley rats have gotten so bold they're
gnawing at kitchen windows in the stealth of the night
cause it's so hard to find good garbage.

Listen Bozo, pull off that clowndisguise:
can't you hear nobody's laughing at your lies?
we all see your ringmaster's draped in a Dracula cape
and we all know the cackling
that makes the walls shake so
every time you cross your eyes or fall flat on your face
is only blasting over the loudspeaker
from an old Nixontape

but you won't make your escape
Even now in a smokechoked vault
beneath the center ring,
cold drops of sweat dribble down your fatboys' necks
as they ante up their stakes
glances roving behind their backs
shaking fingers can barely hold the cards,
they know the hour's late but
still each can't resist the thrill
of trying to make one last killing
before trying to slip away into the dark

but we've got the trapdoor locked,
the secretpassage blocked and
Up here in the sullen glaring crowd
the hawkers have thrown away

their venom cotton candy,
ushers' uniforms and guards' tin stars
litter the aisles,

from the control booth high above
crashing echoes chill the night
any minute, Pres, *our* guys will flip on all the lights.

Then we'll see if the clown can smile.

THE LAW

There's businessmen who work this side the law
and businessmen
who work that:

vultures who like light meat
vultures who like dark

WALLSTREET AND MAFIA ARE ONE
MONEY IS THEIR ONLY LAW

they pick apart our bones together with the same poisonous breath
nest in the same lurking fog

PEOPLES LAW
PEOPLES WAR
PEOPLES JUSTICE

WATCHING THE TV NEWS

Down south there's "banana republics" they say,
where highheeled generals sip blood through plastic straws
where union bosses tapdance and newsmen do pratfalls
where the election booths are draped in widows' shawls

Down south there's "banana republics" they say,
where party platforms paper the walls of buzzards' lairs
where shadowed eyes keep constant watch through crosshairs
where the fruit trees are fertilized with workers' short lives
where plantation owners and their wives have sordid little
affairs

But up north there's a gringo republic I know
where highheeled generals sip blood through plastic straws
where union bosses tapdance and newsmen do pratfalls
where the election booths are draped in widows' shawls
where party platforms paper the walls of buzzards' lairs
where shadowed eyes keep constant watch through crosshairs
where the machines are fertilized with workers' short lives
where stockholder husbands and wives have sordid little affairs

So who's calling who a banana?

Who ties a black silk bandanna
over his face when he makes housecalls?

Who writes all the secret knocks
for the Fatboys in the Tower
and hands out the false promises and poison rings
in the Multinational Chamber of Horrors?

Who elects himself every year Chairman of the Board?

Who can't walk down his own street
unless well guarded by his secretsecret police?
and
who's always met with ungrateful servants
picketing his front door?

Who's the biggest banana

yeah the biggest
banana of them all?

SIDE TO SIDE

Man my feet were getting tired
stomping this picket line;
glad we're all here now
and it's getting near high tide;
hey grab a sign and a handful of petitions:
it's a good day to liberate our working conditions!
just in time!
Fly the Workers Militia:
solidarity can ease your mind
solidarity can ease your mind

Man those bulls must be wired
up on shoeshine polish and sweet wine:
they'd rather crack your skull
than tell you the correct time.
I ain't scared and I ain't superstitious
but momma always told me bullshit ain't too nutritious
ten's my unlucky number
and they already tried to crack me nine times
But now I'm Workers Militia and
solidarity pays for your fine
solidarity pays for your fine

Man I feel like a choir
singing halleluiah to the sky;
I'm gonna take my pain
and bake it in a blackbird pie.
I ain't sorry and I ain't malicious:
even grandma said that judgment day
was gonna be delicious,
and just look at them uniforms
running for a place to hide!
Fly that Workers Militia
solidarity sways side to side
solidarity sways side to side.

FORGET/REMEMBER

FORGET/REMEMBER

forget cats purr through their veins
forget this is a tunnel of glass
forget waving to mommy from the merry-go-round
forget entering the house of your inner nature
forget the second time you fell in love
forget handfuls of moist earth
forget no one won the war
forget it's only a mirror to your own light
forget to kiss your mother goodbye
forget this infinite eternity
forget you're not the first person to say that to me
forget to comfort your lover
forget you were given this gift to guard
forget it is a long way into the poem
forget the smell of autumn leaves
forget swearing you'd always remember that moment
forget when you had all the time in the world
forget new snow by early morning light
forget the clouds opening sweetly like knees
forget to be nice to the grass
forget this most perfect fire opal
forget the feet of the notyetborn
forget this does not belong to only you
forget accepting the pain
forget the chief executive officer will not be eligible for parole
forget the pigeons are listening
forget you are a direct descendant of the first spark of life
forget to forgive the ones you don'tlove
forget to forgive the ones you love

remember cats purr through their veins
remember this is a tunnel of glass
remember waving to mommy from the merry-go-round
remember entering the house of your inner nature
remember the second time you fell in love
remember handfuls of moist earth
remember no one won the war
remember it's only a mirror to your own light

remember to kiss your mother goodbye
remember this infinite eternity
remember you're not the first person to say that to me
remember to comfort your lover
remember you were given this gift to guard
remember it is a long way into the poem
remember the smell of autumn leaves
remember swearing you'd always remember that moment
remember when you had all the time in the world
remember new snow by early morning light
remember the clouds opening sweetly like knees
remember to be nice to the grass
remember this most perfect fire opal
remember the feet of the notyetborn
remember this does not belong to only you
remember accepting the pain
remember the chief executive officer will not be eligible for
parole
remember the pigeons are listening
remember you are a direct descendant of the first spark of life
remember to forgive the ones you don'tlove
remember to forgive the ones you love

CROWS

Hiroshima and Nagasaki may seem
over a half century away
but, I'm sorry to say,
what goes around is coming around
while all around us
crows are flying home to roost
though few have even noticed.

Not long ago Americans shot
"spent" uranium bullets
which weren't really very "spent"
against Iraqi tanks.

While even now American missiles
kill and maim daughters and grandfathers
around the world.

The Pentagon still claims
they don't know
why thirty thousand young Americans
came home mysteriously sick from
the Gulf.

Could it just be because
what goes around is coming around,
while all around us
irradiated crows are flying home to roost
and Atomic War Two has already begun?

A LEAF TWIRLING

A leaf twirling in a spider web,
pelicans dive headlong into the sea:
I wouldn't begrudge it to you, honey,
don't begrudge it to me.

Silent on a mountaintop
the cracks in an old wooden fence
dandelions in the school yard
a baby smiles at a cockroach
the guitar string breaks but the music streams on
she slowly lowers the jaguar mask
look! up in the sky!
the veins in a live oak leaf
the pains of betrayal
the discovery of electricity while
touching a knee
when I listen at least she speaks
if you know the truth why can't you sing it to me
Gorbachev watches fireflies at dusk
an old friend across the street
I brush your earlobe with the tip of my tongue
the hat you wore on your sixth birthday
what is washing a dish between a woman and man
why are we all in the penitentiary
why do you smell different than you usually do
at 5 am I hear you turn the key
remember that feeling is everything
I wouldn't begrudge it to you, honey,
don't begrudge it to me.

SPLINTERS OF MIRROR

Splinters of mirror shattered on the floor
barbed wire screwed into your brain
the muffler bounces across the highway
the urinal is full
pitbulls only follow orders
why can't you help me
ease the pain
we must
we must become indigenous again

now the president paces in a teak-paneled room
the lawyer keeps his eye on the deck
a tenant writes a check he prays is good
a homeless prophet prays for Robin Hood
down by the bus stop a woman
decides to seize her own fate
beneath the concrete a seed quietly waits

why don't we just
ruminate together
your graduation picture still exists somewhere
between the lake and summer's end
you had a friend with frizzy hair
the scent of new-mown hay
I'll show you what is in my hand
if you come with me
to Camagüey
listen closely you can hear
the creek that once flowed
not far away
we must
we must become indigenous again

EARTHQUAKE UNDER THE OCEAN

earthquake under the ocean
the pain the rocks feel
the mind refuses anything at all
a hawk on the corner of your roof
the hand is only asking for a dime
in the eyes of a fleeing wolf

you climb a precarious trail beside a waterfall
risk your heart on the fall of a card
turn a corner on a moonless night
run a race you have no chance to win
touch a shoulder that's kept its feelings unspoken
kiss the palms of a woman who's worked hard all her life
rush out to see the dawn
look into the eyes of a spirit unbroken

a flower choosing to open
take off your innermost disguise
roots delve bedrock deep
penetrate your heart in search of sleep
a potted plant wondering where to go
the river deciding which way to flow
six hummingbirds hover above your head
it's a law of the universe:

grow or die

MARRIES

bumblebee marries meteorite shower
midnight sky marries dandelion
ice floe marries redwood sprout
solar flare marries sea lion
pile of autumn leaves marries
do you have a free night
you're kind of cute marries
sap of a pear tree
your lips are the full moon marries
you think you're always right
I hope you'll come back soon marries
you care more about him than me

hummingbird outside of your window marries
tear open your heart
accept the things you hate most marries
compassion for a shark
show me all your blemishes marries
why can't we be friends
you don't ever say you're sorry marries
nothing you can do will ever make amends
to prove your point you'd sit in a hole marries
it used to excite me to thrill you
I trust you as far as I can throw your soul marries
if you do that again I'll kill you
predictable but not reliable marries
our lives just aren't healing
it's worse than being alone marries
why are you so afraid of feeling

fingers touching rabbit marries
on your elbows and knees examine a clover
giving milk to a tabby cat marries
our lives are almost over
put on your oldest shoes marries
sitting on a bench in the park
whatever happened to your first doll marries
walk across a bridge in the dark

go ahead you know how marries
call me real soon
respect for the grass marries
dancing under the moon
grow old with friends marries
bellywop on a flexible flyer
forgive yourself for being human marries
hold the obsidian mirror up before the fire

THE DOLL OF A HOMELESS GIRL

Mannequin in the mirror
insane banker under the bed
Goddess in a straightjacket
tearing off her head
Let's get perspective on it:
hail bounces against the roof
a wedding march for the dead.

Disillusioned revolutionary
betray what you hold most dear
Bleeding woman needy man
do whatever pleases your fears
Let's get perspective on it:
nothing is ever whatever it appears.

River rat lame excuse
is a prophet with his hand in your pants
The president when no one follows orders
is a puma crouching on a branch
A sea lion eyed by a shark
is the spirit of ceremonial dance
Let's get perspective on it:
morning dew
takes a desperate chance.

The dog of another world
is your lover causing you grief
That thing you clutch in your mind
holds communion with a false priest
Let's get perspective on it:
the doll of a homeless girl
blows the conch shell on a deserted beach.

THREE QUESTIONS

Three Questions
Regarding the Proposition
that
For Every Action
there is an Equal and Opposite
Reaction

Question One:
What is the most recent use
of nuclear weapons in war?

Question Two:
Who is the largest importer of
coca into the US?

Question Three:
What will you find
under
an old board lying
on the grass?

If you answered Hiroshima or Nagasaki
to Question One,
What is the most recent use
of nuclear weapons in war?
you were wrong:
In fact, the US Army
shot uranium bullets
at Saddam Hussein's tanks.

If you answered narcotraffickers
to Question Two,
Who is the largest importer of coca
into the US?
you were wrong:
In fact, the largest importer of
coca is the Coca Cola company,
importing over 500 metric tons
of Bolivian coca leaves each year,

from which it extracts
what it terms
on the Coke label
"natural flavors."

As to the Answer to Question Three:
If you see
an old board lying
on the grass,
and lift it up
what will you find
under it?

An equal and opposite reaction.
Try it and see.

NATIONAL SCIENCE

Livermore National Science Laboratory
Death classified fusioning laser antiballistic
biomass genomelt thermowar Livermore
nevermore
The night of the quarry hides sobbing in brambles while
children writhe begging for absolution Livermore
nevermore
My love makes a vow she will bleed in the ocean till
statesmen's lies corrupt crescent moonrise Livermore
nevermore
Father forbids the limp of the morning fissioning scars
scalpel chastisement the stars secret hornets Livermore
nevermore
Paper cars on TV poisonous ashes of doom whistle the stealth
of assassins in priests' smiles Livermore
nevermore
Laundrymats whining for penance doubtful saviors at
ulcering slashes of greed in the hillside Livermore
nevermore
Death classified fusioning laser antiballistic
biomass genomelt thermowar Livermore
nevermore
no more Livermore
NO MORE NATIONAL SCIENCE

GREEN FLOWERS DRIZZLE DOWN

Green flowers drizzle down
corn tassels of copal incense,
pine seedwings blow from the conch of gold,
scatter with each beat of the quaking house,
we lose ourselves in these flowers
entering beyond, in the jade
drum flower
the sky passing through those buds
falling pleasure as
life is infinite
the aroma of wind on these lips
in the room of bracelets
the air redolent with pollen
the dance wind beside the drum
waving your green plume fan
uttering these stamens
our pain subsides
we whirl asleep in petals of dream
these holy buds bloom!

EYES VISUAL

eyes inner eyes outer eyes sensual eyes
spiritual eyes mental eyes aural eyes visual eyes
spray foam on a breaker's crest
your lover trusting in you
the foreskin of an elk
Jupiter moves past Neptune
you think with your open heart
a pebble drops into Lake Michigan
those pants have a hole in the knee
the duck decides to walk backwards
polished nails fumble with a zipper
the stockmarket dives into a submerged obstacle

eyes inner eyes outer eyes sensual eyes
spiritual eyes mental eyes aural eyes visual eyes
they extract ice needles from the commander's favorite mirror
the governor's wife reveals her taste for schnauzers
the chairman reaches for his hair die but picks up the hot sauce instead
the autopsy reveals choking on lies
the election returns him over to the hyenas
Ronald Reagan on his death bed, the look on his face when he realizes that
Augusto Sandino is waiting for him on the Other Side

eyes inner eyes outer eyes sensual eyes
spiritual eyes mental eyes aural eyes visual eyes
the scent of your lover in the morning
it's on the tip of your tongue
six reasons for not committing suicide yet
a young giraffe has her first period
you rise to the occasion
Mary, in her dream, discovers Harry's hand
your boss and landlord caught at the border
mother wades into the ocean
private ownership of land is hereby abolished
yourself in a sphere of flames.

COLORWHEEL

sunset clouds over halfmoon bay
a fox peers out of a bramble
a patch of snapdragons sheltered by a dune
a parrot ruffles its neck feathers
the deepest spot in a tropical lagoon
twilight in a valley after a cold fall day

red orange yellow green blue violet red
orange yellow green blue violet

red as the stains on a stock certificate
orange dry leaves on a shallow grave
the yellow skin of a starving child
gangrene in a prisoner's leg
the president's veins bulging with lies
as violet as a row of patriots rotting away

fiery lettering on picket signs
a freckle on your lover's chin
you dig in a hillside of pale moist clay
buds burst forth from a branch that looked dead
uniforms scatter at the break of day
as violet as a tornado twisting fences away
COLORWHEEL

SMILE

"In our new society the people must help each other.
If they do that, they'll feel better." Mao Zedong, 1944

Why bother
with a revolution at all
if it 's not going to make people feel better?
Or, conversely, Is it really
The Revolution
if it doesn't make The People
feel better?

A lot of people in the USA
don't feel good.
How much of that
is the social system? How much is
the human condition? Does the Supreme Court
have jurisdiction to decide?

Does cooperation and mutual aid in fact
make people feel better
than competition? Does "socialism"
make a society
feel better than
"capitalism"? This
is ideological struggle! And what
about "anarchism" and "Islam"?
Let's get down to details!

If we had a
pleasure meter
that recorded how good or bad people felt the world over,
what would be the results? Could we measure
progress and reaction
by shifts of a pleasure needle ?

Could we know how much
"freedom" or "socialism"
was in any particular place
at any particular time
by how high it scored on the

pleasure meter?

Would the most “free” or
most “socialist”
place on earth
be the one with the highest score?

How would Havana rate beside Las Vegas?
A collective farm outside Santiago
beside a factory near San Francisco Bay?
What if Minnesota scored
about the same as the Ukraine
but lower than the Basque region of Spain?

I recently
read an article that proposed
we all practice smiling
a few times each day.
I must admit
I checked it out.
As soon as I got the hang of it
I felt much much better.
Now I laugh a lot of the time.
When anybody asks me why,
I tell them it's because I
'm a revolutionary.

VOWELS

O - I - E - A - O - I - E - A
I - O- A - E - I - O- A - E
O- A - E - I - O- A - E - I
A - E - I - O - A - E - I - O

vowels in the control room demanding equal pay
vowels at the executive club carrying graft on a silver tray
vowels find you in the barn and we tumble in the hay
vowels are very strange in the eyes of a bluejay
vowels by your lover's pillow kissing a dimple on her fantasy
vowels in the pouch of a jumping wallaby
vowels beneath the bark of a sugar maple tree
vowels join a garage band outside of Cincinnati
vowels in a jail cell with truth inside her thigh
vowels in a sunken city watching squids glide by
vowels wonder if politicians feel guilty when they lie
vowels in the afterglow of a firefly
vowels in the garden leaning on a magic hoe
vowels on the river bank watching the pebbles flow
vowels on the courthouse stairs spraypainting the word NO
vowels fly across the border upon a laughing crow
vowels atop a pyramid without one shoe
vowels slide down a tunnel to Timbuctu
vowels slips off her jacket and shows you her clues
vowels arm the people with meadow morning dew
you sit by a waterfall and gaze on through
and sometimes know why.
Because of VOWELS

HOW DO WE KNOW OUR INALIENABLE RIGHTS?

We don't know them
by reading the Declaration of Independence
We don't know
them by asking the lawyers

Self-evident truths are
innate in the mind;
They drop
as if from the skies,
beyond argument, reasoned
or unreasoned. Do slaves
need to debate
their right to rebel?
Has workplace
democracy been denied?

And what about the Laws of Nature
and of Nature's God?
Consider the mountain meadows
and the caribou.
Is social justice
inconvenient?
Here
in the course of human events…

THE DRY SPACE BENEATH THE WATERFALL

Why aren't poets on live network TV?
because poetry is boring
you can't understand it.
The dry space beneath the waterfall
the sky wears a green bathrobe
before you climb the scaffold remember your level
yesterday we kissed the earth many times
teak wood is the skeleton of the teak tree
how I love to snuggle your footsteps
crystal fragments shatter across the floor,
burying your heart down the deep twists of tomorrow,
while an entire generation of young men,
mostly brown and black on low-level drug charges,
have quadrupled and quadrupled again
the prison population in the last twenty years
and many tens of billions of dollars more are poised
today to pour like reinforced concrete
into even more prisons and police,
while the CIA and international banks
are the ones who really run the drug trade
and why aren't
poets on live network TV?
because poetry is boring
you can't understand it
and you never know what a poet might say.

RIDE THE WIND

a poem cycle in 16 parts

INVOCATION

The Changes slide ten thousand years,
urging dawn from yesterday;
Revolution spirals ten thousand years,
but what great surges we can stride today!

1

CLOUDS SWIRLING ROUND MOUNTAIN PEAKS

Clouds swirling round mountain peaks
the hole in the center of the sun
girl and boy eyeing each other at a dance
bird hanging from barbed wire
landlord collecting neutron bomb
arm being pulled off by machine
profit graph impaling elk
ward off corporate bubonic spell
organize forest picket slaughterhouse
pull off president's hood
push banker to assembly line
grass returning to laughter
prisoners healing sunrise
ocean flesh filling with pleasure
gong singing compassion.

2
MOLD IN THE SEED POD

Mold in the seed pod
three lawyers peeking from pockets
copcars parked in dark alleys
the space between you and me
dreaming this storm of grief
the gun behind the income tax form
ocean wave fleeing from oilslick
tv shows feeding your cancer
block Rockefeller inflation kick
gnaw termites tax shelter foundation
tear down Business As Usual sign
stars wander through your organs
these fingers down your spine
the reflection of willows in a pond
paper airplanes glide to the moon
releasing comet bliss

3
SMOKE FROM A MINDFIRE

Smoke from a mindfire
running to meet your love
sliver moon over the desert
dragonflies swoop with joined genitals
the circulation of bloodmoney
preservatives clumping in brain tumor
spider on Nixon's wart
white sugar radiation sickness
cattle prod in your eye
hook up Dick Cheney to live detector
cancel insurance companies
hurl brick at computer card
sail to Zanzibar
lick tongues with a spirit
humble yourself before a bird
the heart in your secret pocket

4
THE MOMENT BEFORE SUNRISE

The moment before sunrise
galaxies in the eyes of a wolf
armored car trucking food to supermarket
the lock on a layoff slip
Batman in the service of finance capital
two dogs lying to each other
bedbugs on a cell wall
kick time clock
dodge Bank of America lies
flooring foreman bad energy
neutralizing money acid
a bonfire of rifles
Bush caught trying to swallow evidence
food moon stars
the universe breathing thanks
the axis of the cleansing madness

5
RUNNING THROUGH PILES OF AUTUMN LEAVES

Running through piles of autumn leaves
billows of smoke from an extinct volcano
moonrise in a dark closet
the lock on the toilet door
all that was better left unsaid
your landlord writing in fine print
sobbing through the stillness
ducking tear gas canister
fold compúter programmer
biting snitch's tongue
three bosses running
flooding the caves beneath the pentagon
ducks rising from the foam of a wave
the stumble of a lizard
he inside of your lover's thigh
giving away something you love

6
THE WALL BEHIND THE MIRROR

The wall behind the mirror
condors circling Brooklyn
the wind between sleep and waking
sparks spinning from a galaxy
pus dripping from a factory
the hard lump behind the eyes of a cop
the hand slapping your pleasure
broken angels marching lockstep into nightmare
disarming drill sergeant curse
rip off FBI agent's mustache
jump out of crashing car
evacuate corporations
vacuum the floor of congress
recongregate peach orchards
look deep into an old person's eyes
scatter summer showers

7
TREES TURN UP THEIR LEAVES

Trees turn up their leaves
talking to your honey long distance
the ocean floor glows and splits
rain approaching from the desert
concrete funneled into your mouth
politicians gangbanging an antelope
a parking meter punctures your heart
your casket waits at the end of the employment line
tear up overcharge
fog general's sunglasses
rent increase storm strike
checkmate bank guards
stockholder wringing mop in scrub bucket
thank you energy swirl
gliding up an endless banister
the torch in my stillness

8
FURNACE SPIRIT ARISING

Furnace spirit arising
earth bowels speak mountain geyser
cattle turn their heads into the wind
running sores across the forest
plane poisondusting prairie dog city
popradio smiling newslies
the smell of plowed fields after rain
evict land speculator
turning assembly line money tide
elbow in J.P. Morgan's stomach
ripping up national debt
scab fenceposts falling
crickets chant moonrise fullness
neighbor hugging flowers
the voice in the flowing metal
cutting barbed wire

9
LIPS ON THE VERGE OF TOUCHING

Lips on the verge of touching
forest walking into night
the soul of music in the space between your hips
bison stampede into a snowstorm
dirty socks on the foodstamp line
sniffinglue on sale
the chains heavy on your ankles
stockholders dancing round a fart
frisk cop
roll up boss' eyes
trucking food to strikers
unslicing corporate pie
abolish money with love
sky energy flow through my thankful hands
god in the mind of a child
coming in your lover's soul

10
ELATION OF PUBIC HAIR

Elation of pubic hair
the lights of the inner city
calling the sunrise
your mother's lap
munitions factories vomit in reservoirs
layoff slip reeking cancer
copclub shatters the bridge of your nose
flesh dream time
jumble numbers on bank ledgers
kicking profit margin into ferns
neighborhood committee blocking eviction
grocery clerks handing out food
rabbit tending the fire
the universe in a raindrop
whales spout off a misty island
this offering to tomorrow

11
FROM THE SECRET IN THE MARROW

From the secret in the marrow
hawks in a treetop
watching the banks of underground rivers
the numbers on your ballot
sorrow of the ocean
knife beneath your thumbnail
boss giving you an order
deflect poisoned arrow
medicine song burn mafia fungus
indigestion toothache Newt Gingrich
ink vanish on search warrant
strike lightning in the same place twice
twelve bankers panic in a circle
tree thanking rain
a grove of blackeyed susans
the fingers of a tiny baby

12
THE FACE IN THE FIRE

The face in the fire
yellow sprouts turning green
wild horses in the clouds
that offering look in your eyes
the law against whatever you're doing
blood on a cop's shoe
bulldozer crashing through caribou herd
jets strafe ghetto
nuclear wastes seeping into grass
graveyards circle the factories
the time of the gangster-kings
tearing incorporation paper
taking control of tv station
repainting cop car
feeding rabbit
giving gratitude to the sunset
smiling the stillness
breathing the wind

13
THE REVEALINGS OF LAZARUS

The revealings of Lazarus
hardhat in a snake web
neutron missiles forest the moon
firstgraders chorusing allegiance
a bayonet twists in your silence
clover embryo push against seed shell
six tenants talking leaflet
hand knead dough bondage
coyote turning compost pile
sunburst through coma
Trilateral lice swarming
dust clog machinery
four thighs sinking spinning
rainbow tie around smokestack
workers controlling machinery
the houses belong to the residents
city hall purified by cellos
putting to rest the screaming ghost of Buffalo Bill

14
PULSING TOGETHER IN LOVEBLOOD

Pulsing together in loveblood
the mind in a tree root
beansprout stretch arms energy
telling your lover everything
poison slipping through the skin of a peach
all the lies you memorized for history tests
the asskicking room in the police station
demonstrate mountain power
burning slavery contract
defoliate money forest
deflating landlord's stomach
cream face pie card
workers seizing dawncrash
Rockefeller soul sobbing forgiveness
factory breathing grass
rain spine opening
scar tissue heal
moon roll close to sun
energy spinning calmness web
sand release spring water

15
THE CRYPT BENEATH THE CLOSET

the crypt beneath the closet
CIA agent slipping into white gloves
bluebottleflies in a corpse's mouth
the smog of burning hair
corntassels flutter with twilight
mountains open their eyes
being true to your honey
blackcheek whitecheek brushing
punching Reagan's spirit-body
starlings storm Wall Street secret army
dying rats carpet the White House lawn
mist rusting rifle
heart canals overflow armory
unlocking Chamber of Greed
squirrel returning to treefork
singing glows from your breasts
hummingbird hover by lily
drenched in joyful dance
oakleaves fall into a swift river
darkness vanish from the heart of the KuKluxKlan

16
GIANT ROLLING WAVES

Giant rolling waves in the middle of the ocean
cosmic winds whirl
glacier root slide across the pole
cloud descend in an unknown valley
opening a new island in your mind
herd of elk sniffing asbestos factory
broken teeth bounce in the gutter
crosshairs following candidate
knock on your door at four a.m.
Confiscating corporate inventory
draining swamp around stock market
national guard joining strikers
the politicians' last swindle
carpenters run through the Senate
forest fading into jewels
bear wander through prison ruins
workers collective selecting foreperson
Purgation of dawn metal
smile into the great calm
flocks of hearts flying home
Community absorb corporations
inside this circle of fire.

COSMIC ATHLETICS

SPRING WATER

spring water trickles down vaginal hair
the bumps on your lover's nipples
the last time you told a lie
love letters of a sixteen year old girl
your mother's inhibitions
a kiss on each ridge all the way down your spine
cartoon characters laugh and punch each other's face
smoke from a burning flag
the king of Chicago hiding in Argentina
back at your old high school the principal has a crush on his
body guard
the airports spit barbed wire
the streets are paved with turpentine
all the lovers trying to get it all in before
the bankers and lawyers are shooting each other
and here comes Orwell's 1984

they're doing skin searches on the corner
you run your tongue along a sweet fold of skin
Rockefeller claims capitalism brings social justice
your lover's spirit flaps against a window of your soul
the highway turns to flaming blood
you open the curtain, beyond your neighbor's roof
a shimmering object rises and soars
they're serving vulture stew at the stockmarket
they're giving away the food at the supermarket
they're hurling bricks through bank windows right on target
beauty queen's teeth are brown
evil clowns in judges' gowns
businessmen are falling down
the children are singing of the resistance
provocateurs trying to start a race war
seven major cities on general strike
and here comes Orwell's 1984

WHO ARE YOU ANYWAY

two deer jump through an emotion
a snapdragon bends beneath a bee's weight
you turn a corner and meet your shadow
mommy I'm afraid of the dark
reading a William Blake poem out loud
you got a bad grade on your report card
sapwood encircles a douglas fir
childhood in the house of trauma
a spiral of mayflies above a stream
you try to conceive of your mind
stop playing with yourself
those electrons spinning in your armpits
sitting around depressed
cops charging picket line
the guard strolls past your cell
the ribs on your back remind me of a young antelope
these lines change with the seasons
they're strapping you down to the table
you watch your lover take a bath
sharing this bread and cheese
who are you anyway what is this place what'll we do now?

rubbing elbows with the neighbors
look at that pretty girl
this is going down on your permanent record
no boss I won't do it
your lover isn't your truelove
you deserve better than this
hurling back teargas canister
workers militia stopping scabs
you take the club away from a cop
national strike committee shuts down the highway
emeralds bounce against buttocks
neighborhood committee tearing down fences
ex-banker shuffles on the employment line
watering the garden you swim through your lover's chest
kissing your beautiful stretch marks
your lover really is your truelove

you gaze into a weathered face and see a child
who are you anyway what is this place what'll we do now?

a peach drops from a tree
the circle of our lives
tiny kisses on your breasts
fire blows through your navel
seed looks for a spot to put down roots
you make love to a wind
earthshadow move slowly across moonvalley
an old man plays with a puppy
we owe each other a living
the reconciliation of the packs
snake sheds its skin
stepping through a stone into the wind
moon energy birth shine
the tribe climbs through a cloud into a new world

BECAUSE

because of the moon through the branches of the trees
because you slipped out of your dress
because this shopping center was once a hollow
where at dusk whippoorwills sang
because the teacher said so
because of the shine in an infant's eye
because your hips feel like waterfalls
because they don't care what else happens as long as they get
theirs
because if you sit here very quietly redtail deer will walk by
because my mouth is filled with you
because there's a universe under every fallen log and a
wilderness under every flat stone
because hungry hearts prowl the streets of dream
because they're tattooing the seaturtles with sulfur
because you don't want to lose what little you've got
because talking on the telephone too much can give you cancer
because madrone trees don't lie
because the atmospheric ozone layer is worth more than
deodorant
because Kickass rules the world
because these handcuffs are bleeding
because they installed a tiny microphone inside your ear
because an American factory is almost a perfect miniature of a
fascist state
because of the markings on this ring
because you and I are only now and here
because a bird doesn't care about its scientific name
because these symbols scare the bribes off judges
because employees and tenants are in bondage and bondage is
supposed to be abolished in America
because these plums know exactly when to blossom
because this is neither this nor that and that is both that and this
because you were born to walk this picketline
because every pore of your body is a star
because worker collectives can do a better job running the
industries than bankers' henchmen can
because willows love to watch the ripples in a quiet pond

because we want to abolish their power not kill them or become
them
because our minds when left to float free always point north
because overthrowing the government and overthrowing the
dictatorship are not at all the same thing
because socialism without democracy isn't socialist and
democracy without socialism isn't democratic
because in a mountain glade somewhere a yellow bird is
warbling
because even Richard Nixon was once a beautiful baby
because consciousness purifies
because you can find the answer by looking very closely in your
garbage can
because if you'll just wipe the blood from your face and climb
back to your feet
you'll fall helplessly hopelessly in love

AMERICA A MIRACLE

your lover is very sick
the manufacturers' association writes a new law
the cop orders you to show your i.d.
someone has dumped garbage on our mountain
a row of skulls guards the tunnel to the vault
brown paper bag being handed to labor racketeer
hailstones hit the streets of Cincinnati
a green grasshopper rubs its antennae
four-year-old tying shoelace
music envelops a maple tree
worm eating its way through the soil beneath your feet
a wind stretches your innermost muscles
these words vibrating between our brains
a gull looks down into a prison yard
clouds tumble past the setting sun
the crickets are suddenly quiet

this miracle

crown of a head pushing out through vagina
your grandmother's last words
two tongues encircle a comet
something is happening under the boardwalk
you wake up in a dream
you find a poem in a sandwich
baby watching bug on yellow weed flower
spirits ride the rings of Saturn
the way you look on the molecular level
two spotted blue eggs beneath a hummingbird
a ladybug flies past your heart's desire
you roll your eyes back and see sunrise
your great-grandmother giggles in the dark
you remember the words to the song
you pass beyond cosmic boredom
you turn your lover over
rain floods a cemetery of timeclocks
a hundred pelicans join the picketline
the phones go dead at the stockmarket

workers rummaging through boss' office
the boardmembers plead insanity
tenants abolishing landlords
rank-and-file committee managing factory
you seize control of your job
the president calls for his mommy
you nestle your lover's nipples like eternity
you rediscover that work can be a joy
continents drifting toward marriage
languages mingle their seed
deer makes love to unicorn
the races go for a hayride
the wind laughs at all borders
the key fits your manacles
you lose all fear you can't stop saying I love you
you step out into the morning

this miracle

RIDDLE FOR A BROWN-EYED CHILD

Sometimes this seems like the strangest story
sometimes my rib cage feels like the sky
sometimes it all seems an allegory
sometimes I can only shake my head and cry
sometimes my room keeps quaking
and nothing is ever what it seems
sometimes the dawn keeps breaking
as I wake from dream after dream

sometimes I feel like a coalminer coughing up my black lungs
sometimes like a crystal deep in an unknown cave
sometimes I feel like a picketline when a wild cat's just lunged
sometimes like a coyote when the moon begins to rave
sometimes like a deaf mute in a dictatorship of the blind
sometimes like a hawk soaring in an infinite mind

sometimes I feel I've been laughing since the first mud began to swell
sometimes I see all history passing in the space between two words
sometimes I feel like a thought being thought by the last living cell
sometimes you change before my startled eyes
into a mynah bird

sometimes I see meaning in the boxcars of a train
sometimes all is sunlight whirling through my shining veins
sometimes I see holy absolution in every shattering of our chains
sometimes I feel socialist revolution in every healing of our mental pain

sometimes I see we are progressing along the fierce immobility of time
sometimes I feel only your nipples pressed like flowers against mine.

BALLAD OF MOM AND DAD

"How could you do it? Don't you love me?
the toilet brush is earthquake-blue rolling its sorrowful eyes on
    the payday line
"I always save frozen orange juice containers to pour off
    chicken fat into."
the cleanser smoked our coffee break
while the bathtub ring is singing melon rinds
"I was seven goddamn minutes late they got no right to dock
    me a half hour."
the speedup is crackling, the gas bill is vicious
"Oooo there are little round shiny bugs in the flour."
"For crying out loud, can't you even wash the dishes?"
the tv weatherman is doing a striptease
the yellow cat snores in a puddle of burning machine grease
the foreman whirls down the drain but a dream drowns his
    screams
Mom is praying to deargod make it stop please
Dad and Mom lie back to back, each hoping the other is asleep

Mommy was a choreslave till it broke her spirit
Daddy was a wageslave till it broke his back
Mommy got shrunk in the broomcloset
Daddy got stretched on the boss' rack
Dad's working nightshift and is hardly ever home
Mom keeps whispering she only wants to be alone
Dad's beside the tv snoring and groaning
Mom's beside herself and won't answer the phone
Dad's got a heart attack and flowers on his stone
Mom's got cancer and you can see all her bones

Remember that evening in the park when you first touched each
    other's cheek?
remember how you slipped and skinned your heart?
remember when she didn't return your call for what felt like
    almost a week?
remember his first fumbling your bra?
remember how your energy fields shimmered almost the same
and drenched your thankful mind in a hot glowing rain?

remember how the grind began to drive you apart?
how you were resigned to servitude three years at most well
maybe five or ten
how you panicked when you saw the gate swing closed
and the prophets of gloom turn out to be the wise,
remember how the lackeys in their cocked silk hats drove
smartly past your pen
while their children sobbed and mocked at you for having
drunk their fathers' lies?

Daddy, I know you only did what you thought you had to do
Momma, where'd you find the strength to pull us through?
Daddy, don't try to stop me I know what I got to do
they ain't going to check-mate me like they trumped all over
you:
all pawns are wild now and so are the knights of hearts
Momma, we got to light candles from the stars

ON PROTECTING OUR EARTH AND SOULS FROM THE PRICE OF BREAD

-1-

put away Their deeds and capital gains
and put them to work tending the trees
and cleaning the drains.
ocean breeze,
smells like rain

-2-

the Democracy of
Money is a curious land
everybody in line
because I told you to
you're going to stay after school
it's for your own good
that's woman's work
your rent will be thirty dollars
more next month
can't you work a little faster late again we'll have to let you go
failure to complywith thiswarning every bodyclear the area
let's seeyour i.d. handsuponthecar if
you don't quiet down we'll have to
give you another injection
"but this isn't direct democracy, this is
representative democracy..."

-3-

inequality among the children: quake
faults slash across the land.
sand absorbing waves, waves
pounding sand.
forbidden by plundering businessmen to share
the necessities of common skies,
gulls gather hills trem
ble valleys groan and str
etch and begin to rise.

DISARMING AMEROSHIMA

sun energy blow from the east
river energy glow from the south
wind energy flow from the west
mind energy drone from the north

the sweetsmell of damp pubes
the first time you ever tonguekissed
your lover giving you a gift
garbage islands drift in the middle of the ocean
chemical fog approaching playground
security guard splithead bloodgutter slum
your boss eyes you suspiciously
bankercancer added to preserve freshness
boardmembers expressing confidence in management
nuclear wastes trickle through cell walls
statistics hiding bureaucrat
fallout hovers over porpoise pod
a leukemia of dividends
ten thousand cows chew radioactive cud
your grandchild plays with her birth defect
Oakland implodes on payday
the suburbs melt into nightmare

picketing moneyplague headquarters
stormriders lifecyclone sit-in
blockade disrupt immobilize
general staff surrenders to forest
energymafia caught at the airport

poisons breaking down into vitamins
spiderwebs glow into clover
missiles blow into forestchildren
reactors drone into turtle nests
financiers flow into plows
the laugh of a week-old baby
your honey's mouth like the beach sun
rabbitfamily goes for a picnic
you fall to earth and kiss your mother

a million old people look up at the full moon
waking in your sweetheart's arms

MARIGOLDS

marigolds drip with dew
dogs sniff each other in a circle
you walk barefoot across clover
a shower of plum blossoms
birds hop in a strange dance
a hippopotamus goes into labor
sunflowers sway in a thunderstorm
flowers are genitals
you disagree about the sexes of a litter of kittens
a rolling wave leaps from your lover's tongue
you wonder if you should say no
your lover plays with your toes
your fingers tremble on a button
you watch the part in your lover's hair
a turtle chomps on a daisy
you hold a succulent in each hand
a rainbow opens before you and the keeper bids you come in
you tickle god under the covers
a morning glory sniffs the wind
bumblebee snuggling black-eyed susan
waterlily watching the clouds
you spear a broccoli bouquet with your fork
flowers are genitals
genitals are flowers

DECADE
a poem cycle in 10 parts

The first Spanish bishop of Yucatan gathered all the Mayan hieroglyphic books he could find, and burned them. The devastation was so complete that only three survived. The Mayas quickly learned the Roman alphabet, and used it to translate hieroglyphic books into alphabetic Mayan. *The Books of Chilam Balam*, filled with astronomy, astrology, mathematics, history, myth, ritual, prophesy, were guarded as bibles by every Mayan community.

YEAR 1

YOU OPEN AN ANCIENT BOOK AND FIND A PRESSED CLOVER

the first day of Spring in Yucatan
would it be
a child wakes up in a coughing fit
would it be
the grandmother bent under her sack
would it be
jaguar walking backward yellow eyes
the moth furls her wings before the ghetto
they forget how to love
singing the unhealing wounds
the puppet glares at the puppet master
rapture the decadent blood
forgetting obsolete distinctions
would it be
lightning bugs appear in your hair
would it be
she spreads her jewels before you on the ground

YEAR 2

THE STONE IS PLANTED IN THE EARTH

comes
the makeupman to powder the leader's cheeks
comes
the heat lightning flashing overhead
comes
the swarming of bees about the exits
comes
the waves crashing against the coast
screams in the night
it will speak in the heart of the rain
when the branches burst into flame
the wooden mask turns and laughs
comes the months run backwards
comes the stepchildren make ready the madness of the time
comes it will speak in the changing of the law
you stand on a mountaintop and watch the clouds

YEAR 3

THE GENITALS BEG TO DISAGREE

on the day
inside the mountain a mouthless cave
on the day
a vaulted room, a silent lake
on the day the darkness is almost palpable
droplets trickle down the rock walls
blind fish, hardly moving
no light reaches this point
wives and husbands do not recall each others' names
they stagger under invisible loads
they mull about the well
on the day
they glance desperately about
on the day
they beg each other for water
your lover taps your shoulder you
remember your dream

YEAR 4

THE HEALING OF OLD WOUNDS
AND THE CREASE OF FRESH SKIN

babies will be born to mothers
in its time
a calico cat will hiss at a chattering squirrel
in its time
the green city will float above the sea of skulls
in its time
caterpillars will eat the bay leaves
orchid buds will suddenly open
sperm as large as salmon will clog the estuary
a little wind will whirl through the squash blossoms
plum branches will push up the eaves
your chest will uncontrollably heave
ants will disassemble the mantis
you take a mouthful of your lover and swallow her pride
echoes of the conversations of birds from a distant time

YEAR 5

CLAY CRUMBLES IN YOUR HAND

this is the time, the mole's teeth
this the corner that does not turn
the mistake denying correction
the chord that refuses to sound
the scorpions defying the crescent moon
fallen is the edge of the sea
fallen the folds of time
horned toads clamor in the crossroads
centipedes swarm out of the grottoes
nations shriek blindly along the jammed freeway
the rule of the burning flies spreads its jaws
you are afraid to open the letter

YEAR 6

WHAT COULD BE EASIER THAN ERASING THE FACTS?

startle
the old men sit, shaking their heads
startle
afraid to speak, afraid to listen
startle
the attack dogs wag their tails
startle
all the pistons have been shot in the head
the music is burned
the sidewalks are removed
snackfood piled rotting in the gutter
the Treasurer books his flight
trampling boots can be heard from the roof
startle
what you're left with after the passions of
youth fade away
startle
the roses swaying in the breeze
suddenly there are no secrets

YEAR 7

THE TREE OF THE SACRED CLOWN

in the time
you ascend the downstaircase
in the time
what has gone before will come again
in the time
shake the rattle of the decade
in the time
the living rock will crack
when the wooden drum is two days sweet
when the word of day is declared
when the burden is bound with compassion
under the command of the precious stones
in the hills of the fatherless the motherless
in the time
the walls will be destroyed
in the time
the house is thrown down

YEAR 8

THEY DO NOT RECALL THE REMOVAL OF THEIR LUST

their feet trample the crumbs
shall it happen
vultures peer out of the courtroom window
shall it happen
press secretaries cough up the evidence
shall it happen
great armadas are sent to stamp out small disobediences
shall it happen
what will we eat?
where will we drink?
when will we take up stones?
startled by the jungle's sexuality
the president soils his pants
shall it happen
the night sky becomes visible above the
innermost city
shall it happen
you climb your lover's body you
dare to pull down the fire

YEAR 9

THEY DISPLAY THE BALLOT BOXES BEFORE THE TV CAMERAS

the colonel's whore reaches for her knife
the last train leaves Washington
beasts roam the desert night at will
the captives chained neck to neck
they cheer the great leader as he waves on by
their noses clipped and bleeding
a time when
children dance in circles of snapdragons
a time when
will anything really be different?
a time when
paying the bills
coyotes at twilight
kisses stolen by a flood of night
a landslide opens an unforeseen

YEAR 10

A NEW STONE APPEARS
A MOMENT OF FIRE

you soar over the city
below are pyramids under construction
robes of flowers and feathers
egrets flock in the red ceiba tree
a crowd is gathering in the great plaza
screech owls and wasps will be implored
when the earth appears in the heart of the sky
you'll stir your lover's rosehips in your favorite cup
the ship will glide perfectly into the dock
what's below will be thrown on high
what's on high will be thrown below
the end will depart
they will lift the jade mask from his face
new beginnings will be revealed
impossible ends will suddenly seem near
this a jaguar said to me

MUTINY

MUTINY

Don't take your chains so personally,
keep them in perspective:
human life will someday cease,
even life itself, all
energy slowing into
nowhen, the universe like
a giant eye closing shut, &
even then, what dreams the universe
might then dream!

Still
now IS
& is
HERE
& that is all
you
& I will ever see
no matter
how many different realities
we may have seen or may see.

And NOW / HERE you & I are chained,
some to the oars &
some in the hold
of a slave galley.
And petty-master swaggers down the row
& flicks his whip
& mutters about how lucky we are
to be free
to choose between
the guard-stalked ship
& the shark-prowled sea
as we patrol
the oceans of the world
in search of booty.
plundering all we meet &
murdering all who would resist.

And each morning the captain
appears on the bridge
in his pin-striped suit
& salutes as the guard
raises the colors:
the bugler blows of stripes & stars
but we fly the jolly roger.

And you & I, poor slaves
in the scheme of all that exists,
what can we do but salute
when we're told, pull our oars,
remember,
be,
& persist
until the world somehow
works through this pain
to some better
eventually?

But deep down we all know
we'll never reach shore
until we mutiny.

BLUE-COLLAR WOMAN

Blue-collar woman,
fire in your arm
& grease on your cheek,
faded red bandanna tying your neck
with a granny knot for a locket;
after a hard day, tough & mean
or smiling like a mountain stream,
rally flier in your jeans,
phillips-head screwdriver
& 15/16th open-ended wrench
sticking out your back pocket:

I just want to tell you
you look fine
driving that 1450 multilith press
clacking & hissing in 4/4ths time,
or rolling on that creeper
beneath that ten ton truck,
arc-welding that ship's truss,
or waving that picket sign.
I just want to tell you
it feels fine
to be hammering with you
on the assembly line,
or pouring concrete forms in rain,
or driving tractors across the plains,
or mopping floors,
or goofing off,
or laughing at the boss,
or shoveling earth for a sewer line.

Because it sure got to feel
pretty weird & unreal
when day after day
& year after year
I was forced to work only with other men.
I just want to tell you
I know it's a hard fight for a working woman

of the working class;
I just want to tell you
you burn like the night
as you twist & weave
in your worker's dance.

IN THE THIRD GRADE

In the third grade
I refused to go to school.
I wandered the streets,
explored the park.
But they caught me
& taught me who was boss,
so I submitted for a while
to their rule.

Later, out on my own,
I had to survive:
I scavenged & hustled
& lived off friends for a while,
till my luck ran out
& I found no recourse
to working for the profit of a boss,
so I submitted for a while
to their rule.

And since then,
I've found myself forced
to submit time & again.

And even now I waste my days
laboring for that crook.

Still, while I drive my aching body
begrudgingly about,
I daydream doing *really* useful work,
to benefit all the people,
& working collectively, democratically
with the others now-enslaved with me
in the shop.
And sometimes this fantasy gives me joy
& helps me get through the day.
But sometimes reality
crashes down on me
like prison bars,
& that crook or his boy

just better not talk down to me
or get in my way.
No, I will not, no
I will not be bought & sold,
& I won't buy, I wont sell.
I'll do what I have to
to survive, but I won't be either a good slave
or strive to be a master;
I will not build a stake
in a system
that condemns the children to war
by depriving most of us
of our rightful share.
I don't mind hard work:
Work, I know, can set us free.
Work is what renews the world
& makes us strong.
Sometimes work is singing.
But slavery just drains our energy
& makes us feel helpless.

I've seen death shut factory gates
& stared at office walls in hell.

No, I am no longer afraid
to strike back at our enemies,
or to speak aloud of sweeping them away:
the worst they can do is kill me
& I've already been through that.

Next time, if I go down,
man I'm going down swinging.

GRANITE CLIFFS

Granite cliffs of cloud, trees like awesome
creatures dancing joyous at the sky out-
side my window, a bird, head & breast red
like fuchsia berries, song ecstatic dark like
the moon:
these energy patterns
we call reality or consciousness
. . . Yet bankers steal our
minds & homes, bosses drink
our souls; they rig things so
money's in charge, hoard our food
in supermarkets, guard our
clothes with burglar alarms, make
lies required reading in school . . .
OUR PERFECT MIND,
OUR BLEEDING MIND!
We may not reconcile, sisters &
brothers, till our consciousness is
pregnant with our longing & our
strength. Then like grass
bursting through cracks in concrete,
this birth in fire . . .

JOE AND TED

Joe's the good cop,
Ted's the bad.
Ted knocks you down,
kicks you in the head.
Joe pulls him off,
helps you to your knees.

"He's crazy, kid,
he'll kill you,"
whispers Joe.
"Do yourself a favor,
tell him what he wants to know,
do like he says."

Cops working in teams
take on roles:
next time
the bad cop'll be Joe.

It's like that
up & down the system:
Our bosses & landlords & the taxmen
are Ted,
the Welfare Department is Joe.

Like every Welfare client knows,
never turn your back on Joe.

ANDY

We needed a sander to keep our shop running;
Andy picked one up at Sears.
But they noticed the bulge beneath his coat
& now he's locked in Santa Rita.

The judge said he was poor once too,
but he'd worked hard & studied;
Andy shuffled from foot to foot,
glanced around & cracked his knuckles.

In the prison diningroom
I sat across from him;
we weren't allowed to touch.
Guards paced expressionless
up & down the rows;
there was so much weeping around us
I could hardly hear.
Beneath the wide table
we touched toes.
Andy said, "There's a lot of us in here."

MY BOSS

My boss stood dawdling
in front of his office,
with a made-up woman in a bright red dress.
As I passed by, invisible to him,
he licked his narrow lips
& displayed one immaculate palm;
the other he kept hidden
in his pants pocket.
"My hands are clean,"
I heard him chuckle.
"Only money making money from money."

Back on the line I tried to work,
but there was grease on my hammer
& fire in my head.
I caught the foreman's eye
& slunk down to the 'head'.
Plunked on the stool,
face in my hands,
& let my weary calves rest.
Then noticed a bent nail
on the crudded floor,
picked it up
& scratched in jagged letters on the wall:

BUT MONEY MAKES MONEY FROM FLESH.

WHO SPEAKS FOR WORKINGPEOPLE?

Who speaks for workingpeople?

"Labor executives"
propped in their chairs
by the bosses
to be their mouthpieces
& keep us in line?

Phony unions make us weak.

Workingpeople's actions speak
for workingpeople.

Organize the unorganized.
Reorganize the mis-organized

I'M ONLY VISITING

I'm only visiting this meat, passing
through it like a child
waking into dream, dreaming into
wake.

Should I
disturb the around?

Water
washes through the
ground
down to the sea, through
mouths of whales &
otters, gills of
fish, then up again, to
clouds.

Still, I
walk these streets, climb these
walls; I see children too
worried to laugh and men
too pained to crawl; they've got
my name on a list down at City Hall.

Should I give them what they ask, make no
distinctions? Change my mind? Or grow
a beard & change my name? Watch us all
sputter blindly to a messy extinction
while my spirit is floating
outside my brain?

If I view this oppression with
distraction will it pass? Or will it just be
me who passes, distracted & oppressed,
while the oppression remains?

DREAMS

They think we're stupid.
They think we should be glad
they let us eat
& walk the streets,
have roofs over our beds;
<u>we</u> know what's going on
inside our heads,
& that's an advantage
we have over them.

Maia told me she dreams as she works,
of ways to bankrupt her boss
as she balances his books.
In Art's dream he cashes his last paycheck,
walks up to his boss,
yanks him by the nose
& dumps him on the deck.
Fred jumps on his boss' desk
and pisses all over the place;
Ann feeds her boss
slowly into her machine;
work stops,
the other workers rush over
in her dream,
to catch the look on the boss' face.

When I was young,
a furrier, Sam,
told a dream to me,
of workers taking over
their places of work,
firing their bosses,
& running things together,
for everyone's needs.
I thought about it a long while,
then (I was 9 or 10)
went up to him & said,
"Sam, if people have got it

so bad like you say,
& we could all have it so good
another way,
why doesn't everybody just do it?"

He said, "People have been trying to,
for a long long time,
& a lot of people have died trying.
It's not just a question
of what's best for the people
or what the people want:
there's guns pointed at us
from all sides."

And now that I'm older
& have worked myself
& dreamed my own dreams & nightmares,
I've learned we all dream the same dreams,
& dreams are powerful beyond compare.
If we can each remember them
& share them,
we can build great visions
out of our despairs,
& visions create surging movements among us
to realize those visions
& dispel our most fearful nightmares.

O CHILDREN

O children,
know that once we children
went away to live among ourselves
in peace among the gentle swaying trees,
stepped through a magic door
to reconstruct our world
in harmony & joy,
expecting all who saw to follow,
the nightmare machine to die for lack of
human parts.

And there we struggled with each other's ghosts
& fears & pains
& tried to work it through
with sharing & with love.

Then slowly we became aware
the screams of burning children
would not fade away beyond the green green hills
but haunted all our songs & dreams;
the sparkling mountain pools,
the silent drifting clouds
were poisoned;
we still huddled from their guns,
bent beneath their laws;
there was no way to not be part:
all is too much tied to all
& too dependent on it.
So one by one we came down
from the soft eternal hills
& stood before the furnace
& the frightful grinding gears,
among the bleeding people
we came back,
O children,
to fight a war.

PERSONAL LIBERATION

Social oppression
has a personal manifestation
that warps & poisons our daily relations,
hurling sister against brother,
lover hurting lover,
dumping on each other
all the shit they dump on us.
Then they try to tell us:
"We're all individually
fucked up & weird."
Either that or:
"It's biological
we're a sick species.
But don't worry, we're evolving:
we might come out of it
(if we're lucky)
in a million years.
So chin up,
make the best of a bad deal."
While psychiatrists fly to the Bahamas
& landlords laugh in their beer!

How can we liberate our personal relations
as long as we relate as boss & wage-slave?
Boss says "do that do this,"
smiles at his own fool mistakes
& throws yours in your face,
pisses away his time
but you better not be ten minutes late,
all the while he's picking your pocket,
aren't those personal relations?

Son of a banker landlord robbing
your food & clothes money
& don't even fix the window or sink,
aren't those personal relations?

You forced to be a petty crook

because you live in a land of crooks,
where the government's the joint dictatorship
of the biggest crooks of all,
& aren't those personal relations?

Or does your personal liberation stop
at who washes the dishes or lies on top?
Or does your personal liberation end
when it's time to punch the time-clock or pay the rent?

Or does your personal liberation end
in a mountain hideout with some close friends?
Or should your personal liberation stop
with privileged organization men & technologists on top?

Why let your personal liberation stop
when liberation is without end?

TECHNOCRACY

Hurtling through eternity,
this
slaveship
earth!
They've seized our means of survival
with their laws & guns & machines,
keep us chained,
some to work them,
the rest to their charity,
desperate, superfluous.

Wherever bosses rule,
technology remains a tool
to keep us in poverty, captivity.

The only breakthrough
that will help toward the solution
is in the technology
of revolution.

DIGGING IN MY GARDEN

Digging in my garden I overturned
a curved flat bone
with a hole in one end
& strange markings its length.
A cry overhead.
I looked up, shielded my eyes.
Three great pale birds veered
southwest, disappeared
into a dark mountain of cloud.

Looking for signs?
Watch the foodstamp lines.
Or where at gunpoint they're giving food away.
One side the bay,
general strike;
on the other side,
armed struggle:
already they're spanned
by a steel bridge.
Who can say
why dark comets pass darkly by,
or where Atlantis might rise?

AS ABOVE, SO BELOW

"As above, so below,"
say the keepers of spiritual revelation.
And so they reign like gods
over their religious non-profit tax-
deductible corporations.
Can heaven really be
an authoritarian class society,
is business God's chosen organization?
What God? The God of Money?
Or is it just the choice
of those anointed
businessmen who peddle god-realization?

But suppose heaven really is
theo-fascist,
God with the face of Nixon,
dressed like the Pope,
talks like Rockefeller
& smells like the Maharaji.
Well then,
don't be surprised to hear
that John the Baptist's back in jail,
and
Jesus is on the streets
crying,
"Struggle, for the Commune is at hand!

BEING NOT SEXIST

Being not sexist
does not mean
not being sexual
(love
is an imperative of meat;
meat is a channel of mind).
Tenderness.

YET DEATH

"Political power grows from the barrel of a gun."

Yet death
is but a wind in the mind.
The clouds change.
(I dreamed only
of generations of birds
then awoke,
still enchained.
Money! Women!
Property!
Bankers bathe in blood
of porpoises & monkeys!
Step right up folks!
Watch the lawyers pick their noses!
See the hula maidens prance!
Soon
I began to think of guns.)
To flow back
to the sunlit whispering hills,
must we first think of guns?
Yet life
is but a wind in the mind.
The clouds change.

SO YOU PICKETED

So you picketed here & rallied there,
& marched through the streets
waving flags & singing,
& got a $100 fine & a couple days in jail
& started to feel
it was all to no avail
when you saw no instant revolution...

Well, you can jump off, brother,
& swear it's the end of the line,
but swear as you will,
this train's moving on!

As long as orphans have to trespass
to survive,
& money decides who gets a hospital bed
& who gets brutalized,
as long as schools regiment to prepare us
for bosses' rule in our jobs;
as long as those who labor are poor
& those who bark orders are rich;
as long as the people are slapped with a choice:
either submit or starve,

THERE WILL BE A MOVEMENT

OPEN, SESAME

How they mindwash our
children's reality, presenting
false images of
freedom & harmony
in a
police-enforced
racist society
where the "game" of business
is just a front
for the dictatorship of money,
& beneath advertising's
happy-day smiles
lurks an incorporated fascist elite,
oh
where is class struggle
on Sesame Street?

MEDITATION

Cast
off your personality, do
whatever occurs to your
brain, see the living crystal
structures of
reality, step out of your
bones & run in the
rain; attune your
energies to the great
streaming frequencies, share your
mind & meat with all
livingkind,
till your body stretches
to the ends of the universe
& the galaxies
are thoughts in your mind . . .
then come back.
And see this day-to-
day reality
where you wipe your ass & wear out
shoes & brains,
is as real, as perfect, &
includes all the rest,
& we don't fully exist outside it.
But. . .
there's
your boss still telling you
what to do, still making ten times
more than you, & for doing nothing, & if
you were to say shit about it, you'd
be fired, then how you going to
pay the rent? still children hungry
cold while stores are piled with
clothes & food. still Reagan,
Rockefeller, Dupont, Mellon, Bush,
Attica, San Quentin, Pepsi-cola, IT&T . . .
Can this be real?
Shut your eyes & hear a oneness in your

body singing; open your eyes &
see this wondrous singing universe;
open your eyes & see we're living
in a corporate fascist state.

Is the road to liberation to shut your eyes again?
Can you stop the slaughter by stopping it
in your mind?
Or must flesh liberate flesh
before mind will reflect it?
Meditation:
a thousand-petaled lotus,
a thousand picket signs.

BUSINESSMEN PADDING

Businessmen padding their paunches,
people desperate in the street,
the economy slowly dissolving,
like a rotten peach.
Yet we must
survive, my sisters &
brothers, so let us
come close, as
close as our wounded souls are
able, breathe
deeply though the sky's not
clear, share
what poor food is left:
with each
other is our freedom, from
each other is our strength.
embryos need
warmth & shadow.
Only if
we cultivate each other
will we harvest.

GENERAL STRIKE

Speedup. Keep moving. No mistakes.

Grin at the boss, tearing a hole
in the side of your stomach worrying
it'll be you laid off
next month or next week.

They tell you to work to get ahead;
you work & work & get deeper in debt.
They tell you our country's the richest
in the world;
the country may be rich, but
tell it to the landlord
knocking at your door.
Recession already taken
next year's vacation,
already digested years of savings,
mounting bills, no pay hike.
A bunch of crooks ruling our nation,
hoarding our wealth,
bleeding us dry:

GENERAL STRIKE!
Kick out the crooks & the bosses!
NATIONAL STRIKE
A shorter work week & useful work for every hand!
GENERAL STRIKE
Produce for needs, not profits!
NATIONAL STRIKE
For control of our jobs
& to take back our homes & tools & land!
STRIKE
STRIKE BACK
against the violence that rules our daily lives!
STRIKE
with every weapon we command!
Like driving rain, overflowing rivers!

NATIONAL STRIKE
For economic democracy!
GENERAL STRIKE!
Until they meet our just demands!

CAN YOU HEAR THE DRONE?

Can you hear the great orgasmic drone
of this wondrous living universe?
Can you hear a million hungry children scream?

Can you see all the lovers in the world
who are making love right now,
feel the planetary pulsations?
Can you see all the lovers in the world
who are being beaten & thrown in jail,
can you taste the guards' humiliations?

Watch that hummingbird
hover by that poisoned rose!
Gaze deep in those damp lilac bushes:
sunglassed generals & tasteful bank presidents
in the shadows
peddling beaver pics
& blood of innocents!

Suppose there <u>is</u> a place beyond,
where none of us hungers or thirsts:
does that mean that therefore it doesn't matter
that here in this place
each day they knock us down,
each day kicked around,
each day worrying about the food & rent,
stick your neck out
& they take you away?

Gaze through the veils of the Kingdom of Heaven.
Gaze through the TV Kingdom of Heroin.

Can you see an act of liberation
in each defiant crime
against corporate property?
Can you see in each picket sign
a strike against the banks' monopoly?
Can you see revolutionary struggle
as spiritual rebirth?

Visualize
a revolutionary comity of neighborhoods and nations
Visualize
a Democratic Communal Earth.

ACUTAPETL

I went up the mountain with Acutapetl:
he led me on a trail I could barely see,
through swamp & over precipice,
across raging streams;
& when I fell & cried I could go no farther,
suddenly he was gone;
I panicked, then pushed slowly on,
& met him by a fallen tree;
his eyes shone like dawn.
He pointed to a boulder
jutting from a grove of thorns,
& said, "Climb it. Tell me what you see."

I saw great forests burning
& animals fleeing,
white fish bellies floating like a carpet
on the sea;
I saw a million bulge-eyed children
throw stones at a wall;
an aged black-shawled woman shoplifting cheese;
I saw fierce explosions in numberless places,
hands drop from arms & walls drop from roofs;
babies & warriors crying in rubble,
numbers tattooed on every cheek;
guards wearing masks patrolling each corner,
tanks rumbling down every street;
I saw corpses in business suits
smile & shake hands
while puddles of blood clotted about their feet.

"Look," said Acutapetl,
in a voice like a bell.
"Tell me what you see."

I saw multitudes surge through the heart
of the city,
men & women sharing the front lines,
I saw police lines dissolve in the people's path,

soldiers ripping off their masks,
some running, some joining
the flash flood of flags & picket signs;
I saw blackmen & whitemen opening jailcells,
people hugging on every street,
I saw great factories run
without bosses or foremen,
millions of children planting trees;
I heard "union" on each lip,
saw communion in every deed;
I saw the ocean quench the planet
& the planet rock the sea;
I saw the planet
as a living conscious entity.

"Look," said Acutapetl,
in a voice like a well.
"Tell me what you see."

I gazed around once more
then down at him, & said,
"I see struggle. I see harmony."

A SPELL AGAINST THE ENEMY

ATHEMA ANATHEMA
SYNATHEMA
H*U*M
the leg of the chair.
conversations in a crowded room.
Rachel's ball.
I am confused.
...death is not the end of it.
yet the pain...
(I see but fear
I am mad, know but fear I am alone)
Che climbs a tree
in Bolivia. Jill walks to the bed.
This is not reality but
the structure of my mind.
she lifts
her dress.
interpretation. yesterday's mind.
To try to conceive
the extinction of consciousness
is thought.
the extinction of consciousness
is not thought.
not-thought.
Still the leaves
darken & crumble, the tide
rolls restlessly in:
caterpillars
with minds of butterflies, butterfly
meatmind in a thousand clustered eggs,
thinking as it has thought without a
break for a million million
years: all that
once set in motion will
sometime find rest, I
know, this pain this
pleasure will finally
resolve for us & for

all (but not for us until
for all), &
resolve when we choose
it. And sooner or later we
will choose it. And then will be
beyond, sensationless, without time
or place, without
person, yes. BUT
THERE & THEN IS NOT YET &
EVEN IF WE HOLD PERSPECTIVE OF THE NEBULAE
& STARS, OF A MILLION MILLION YEARS,
OF THE LIGHT, THE SOUND, OF MIND, OF DREAM,
WE ARE STILL NOW & HERE:
movement, imbalance, struggle,
death, rebirth - these transient bodies, these
fleeting joys, these tears! watching the
changes, being alive within them, part
of them, inseparable from them:
... your thighs soft like the summer sky...
in the ferry bow,
chopping through iceflows, gulls
crying swoop into the churning
wake, your hand in mine, the salt
wind freezes my lips into a smile...
just to feel, to have
bodies that can feel the joy, loneliness, weight
of loving, being loved, not being loved, of
having a mind, a
size, a sex, of growth, of growing old,
in a slave state, a member of an oppressed or
oppressor class.

THOUGH WE MAY EACH HAVE ONCE STEPPED
BLINDLY
INTO THIS PLACE WE DIDN'T CREATE,
WE EACH CREATE IT EVERY DAY.

Sometime we will choose death
again, & it will choose us, I at least hope
to be ready, unattached to this specific vehicle,

anxious to voyage home to be renewed.
Till then
we are together in this body this
mind.
So let us move together
within the movement freely, being
of it, becoming with it, un-
afraid of where that becoming leads, for we can
only flow through, transform, giving seed in
ecstasy & joy, becoming seed ourselves
once more, like birds in the wildness, rain
in the ocean, sunset in the vast night sky,
for it can only lead to clarity:

a handful of millionaires own our land,
industries, resources, control our
government, our lives.

a qualitative rise in our
consciousness will heighten
awareness of our oppression; like a fetus
remembers it's always been both an embryo & a
child, we will remember the embryo we've been,
remember what we are to become.

a mass expansion of our consciousness
can commune our land
resources,
outlaw exploitation,
abolish privilege,
restore the balance,
transform the pain,
recover the lost world.

JUST RETRIBUTION

Criminal financiers crouch in shadows
behind computer spread sheets,
deleting our life savings, our homes,
our future, our nation,
our history
BUT THEY CAN'T DELETE
OUR RETRIBUTION

MASS RETALIATION
PULL OUT ALL STOPS
GENERAL REBELLION
NATIONAL STRIKE

Thunder in the midnight sun!

Restore our stolen rights
Recover our communality
ancient cadences on
a hollow log drum!
Delete the corporations
Reclaim our plundered commons

Past and future merge into one.

HOLES IN YOUR SOLES?

Holes in your soles,
searching for work?
Or boss on your back,
riding you to the floor?
Government a private resort
for hustlers & profiteers,
gamblers stacking every deck,
arming for another war?
Have you had it
up to here?

Well,
if you've ever been bossed at a lousy job,
you don't need a membership card:
just organize among your friends &

FIGHT FOR WORK DEMOCRACY
FIGHT FOR ECONOMIC EQUALITY
FIGHT THE DICTATORSHIP OF PROPERTY
JOIN THE WORKERS ARMY!

INSURRECTION / RESURRECTION

Twenty-two Wall Poems and a Billboard
a poem cycle to battle and help heal

To participate more deeply in the people's movement and to overcome some of my personal alienation, in the early 1970s I wrote this cycle of poems and tagged them on walls around town, the first four with stencils and spray paint. The idea was to make poems telling dangerous truths that aren't often told in public. I signed them with the initials NJ, which stood for Not John. I made the later poems into broadsides which I posted sometimes with wheat paste (like they use for billboards), and sometimes with staples or tape. I painted Wall 22 freehand with a brush. The final poem in the series was a billboard 8' x 12', made of three 4' x 8' drywall panels; a few friends helped me paint it and erect it near the Interstate highway close to the Bay Bridge. It lasted a couple of days before unknown forces reduced it to a pile of rubble. A friend volunteered to fund a small run of the poems in a chapbook, along with photos of them on walls and some other poems, which I published as Insurrection/Resurrection. I prefaced it with the following:

> I've tried to make poems that might be useful to people. If you find any you can use, please feel free. If you just find part of one, use that part & throw the rest away. Change any lines you want. Add others. It's okay with me. If you change one a whole lot, it'll be your poem as much as mine. If you share it with a friend & that friend asks who wrote it, say both of us; if anybody else asks, say anonymous.
> *Not John*

1st WALL: We Build Houses

We build houses, bankers own them;
we build machines, bosses own them;
we try to build our lives,
the government owns them,
and the bosses and the bankers
own the government.
But workingpeople are dreaming
dreams again.
The sky is dark with birds.

2nd WALL: Mr. Corporation

Mr. Corporation: we may slave for you,
but as we slave we're thinking:
We don't need you, we can run things ourselves,
for each other's needs, not your profit.
We know you are afraid of us.
We are an ocean, we are a storm.

3rd WALL: We Work Ten Dollars Worth

We work ten dollars worth, the boss grabs five,
the state steals two: hunger, death,
smoldering Hanoi rubble:
they pervert our work into misery & destruction.
To perpetuate their cheating us.
The unborn children laugh & cry.

4th WALL: They Claim The Ground I Walk

They claim the ground I walk, the
house I live in, the machines I
work at, the goods I produce;
they claim two thousand
years of law behind them &
ten thousand hired men with
guns to back them up & claim
those guns defend their
freedom which they claim is
my freedom too, freedom to
sell them my labor, pay them
my rent, buy back the goods
I've produced, freedom to
scheme to set myself up
like them & exploit fools like
me.
But who am I to
speak?
Just one poor workingman.
And the workers, they claim,
are content.

5th WALL: A Vast Network Of Technology

A vast network of technology,
devised and built by us, capable
of assuring everyone's prosperity:
a few banks control it:
our seas smell of death,
our cities of hunger;
our schools and jobs
are prisons of despair;
our police they own,
our misleaders they choose:
corporations bloated,
survival scarce.
CRIMINALS DICTATE
THE TERMS OF OUR
LIVES: THE ONLY WAY
TO FREE OURSELVES
IS TO UNITE.

6th WALL: HEY KIDS

HEY KIDS
The bankers rule over us.
they steal all the money,
buy the politicians and cops.
They trick us into being slaves,
force us into fighting wars
so they can ransack our world
for their personal hordes.
TELL YOUR FRIENDS
WE ARE GATHERING
LIKE WIND
THIS IS OUR PLANET
THIS IS OUR BLOCK

7th WALL: Dispossessed From Land

Dispossessed from land, resources,
control of our lives, dispossessed
by businessmen:
we were born that way, our children
are being born that way.
THEY'VE STOLEN
OUR FACTORIES OUR
FARMS OUR
GOVERNMENT BUT
THEY CAN'T STEAL
OUR ANGER
We are at war to confiscate back our world.

8th WALL: Our Lives Are At The Whim

Our lives are at the whim
of landlords & bosses:
rents & prices up, wages down, no jobs:
they try to keep us at each others'
throats to just survive.
The night is dark, yes.
But there's many of us
& we're getting ready.
Soon the moon will rise.

9th WALL: When You Can't Stand

When you can't stand
being cheated & pushed around
by your boss another minute,
remember:
in this system
all jobs are like that.
you're "lucky"
to even have one.
They keep the money scarce & the jobs few;
somewhere they got a file on me & you.
THE BOSSES ARE THE
MOB ARE IN POWER
We are chained together.

10th WALL: A Battle, Sometimes Raging

A battle, sometimes raging,
sometimes almost invisible,
in every clothes store, bank,
every supermarket aisle:
this is class war.
We'd like to avoid it, but there's no way;
as long as business owns the law,
we're poorer every day.
Still, we'll get what we need,
one way or another.
WE ARE EACH
OTHERS'
WEAPONS.

11th WALL: Politicians, Bosses

Politicians, bosses, landlords,
leeches bleeding us as they bled
our parents, as they have plans for our kids .
THE PEOPLE ACT TO STOP THEM
they fire, evict us
WE ACT AGAIN AGAIN
they order us beaten jailed murdered
WE ORGANIZE, ACT
ACT AGAIN AGAIN
The leeches are not the only ones with plans.

12th WALL: Broken Shovel

Broken shovel in the sand,
shadows on the slide.
A spiderweb sways between swings.
Today the children stagger home,
disposable surplus of your poisoned war,
eyeless, legless, flesh ripped & sewn.
The grass screams.
Businessman, your game is over.
We're back, full grown, with guns beneath
our soldiers' rags, & are we ever
wise to you.

13th WALL: They Try To Blur

They try to blur
our children's minds with lies, tame
their minds with fear:
they claim to act in our name.
From schoolyard line to battle line
to unemployment line they
march us:
they claim to act in our interest in our name.
THE BEAST IS SLIPPERY -
MANY HEADS & CLAWS, MANY MASKS.
We cannot let ourselves be fooled again.
IT'S TIME WE
ACT IN OUR OWN NAME.

14th WALL: Businessmen Create Our Poverty

Businessmen create our poverty
& perpetuate it, then tell us we're poor
'cause we're stupid or lazy,
Businessmen steal our every
technologic advance & hand us back
unemployment & war,
Businessmen structure fear into our lives to
control us, to cheat us of our equal shares
in this our great grandchildren's earth:
may their violence return to them
like haunting dreams (even now
they are afraid to walk the streets, even
now they are afraid to fall asleep); may
their jail terms be as long
as their bank balances.

15th WALL: When Our Blood Begins To Age

When our blood begins to age,
our muscles slow, our energy retreats
like sap from snow-crisp branches, when
life should begin to mellow:
INTO THE GARBAGE HEAP
expended with, each of us, for
we'll no longer be useful enough
to them, replaced at the office
or machine with fresher, more
profitable flesh.
Then go sit in the park, nothing
in your pocket, or stay home & watch TV
if you haven't hocked it.
The old know the truth: When we're young
they drain our lives into money; when
we're old they help us to get dead.
America is a slaughterhouse.
One by one we're expendable to them.
But together, fighting back
while we've still strength,
we can take care of each other
& expend with them.

16th WALL: We Are A Wounded Mind

We are a wounded mind,
festering, struggling to heal...
"Got to be losers
'cause there's winners,
somebody's got to be boss:
natural selection,"
(the financiers say), "fittest on top."
& you better believe it, kid, &
that's the way it's going to stay, so
keep your ass moving & your mouth shut.
You been lucky so far:
they're still grinning at you they could
come for you tonight!
CLASS STATE IS
POLICE STATE
... a festering wound must be reopened
if it is to heal.

17th WALL: In America

In America there's three classes
(or so they teach in school): a few rich,
the middle class,
and a few poor;
the "middle class" includes most of us, they say,
and we're in control
SUCH MUDDLE IS DESIGNED
TO FRAGMENT US AND SMOKESCREEN
OUR MINDS, DETACH OUR WORDS
FROM WHAT WE SEE, OUR FEELINGS
FROM WHAT WE FEEL.
Our grandchildren will admit
to one another that
so many of us shouted so loud that we were
"free" because we were afraid to
face our slavery.
Money and property rule the people.

18th WALL: Sometimes/ the Pain

Sometimes/ the pain/
of being/ in this prison/
with you . . .
(the warden's owned by bankers,
our bosses are our guards;
property & money are the walls
& the bars.)
Yet even now they're brawling
among themselves, over which
should own our days & nights
& which should rule the mountains & stars.
WE MUST KEEP
STRONG & WAIT & WATCH THE
TOWERS
Soon we will gather in the prison yard.

19th WALL: EITHER YOU GOT A JOB

EITHER YOU GOT A JOB OR YOU
GOT A HUSTLE. IF YOU'RE A
WORKER, MAN YOU GOT A JOB;
IF YOU'RE A BOSS, MAN
YOU GOT A HUSTLE.
How come we got to work for hustlers,
how come they're directing the show?
Why can't
I work for you & you for me,
share what we have, be each other's security?
Did God arrange things like this?
Nature's law, human nature?
Is our collective mind diseased
projecting horrible dreams?
Or am I here alone in my strange creation?
Still, consciousness has laws of its own.
awakening will begin in unbearable
oppression, when death is overcome
power will flow, renewal
(if not for their guns our parents our
grandparents would have kicked them
out long ago).
DAWN.
LIGHTNING FROM BELOW

20th WALL: Crooks Ruling

Crooks ruling our nation,
using inflation
to steal next year's pay hike
& years of our savings!
GENERAL STRIKE!

21st WALL: Poor Blacks

Poor blacks, browns,
Asians, and whites
competing for the same lousy jobs
that aren't even there:
nobody getting a fair share.
So white shoves brown
brown shoves back
black woman blamed
Asian attacked,
huge corporate profits,
poverty biting.
They try to keep us fighting
for crumbs
to try to keep us from
uniting.

22nd WALL: Moving Quietly

Moving quietly at first,
like plants in our coming together.
Sunflowers unfold into clouds of moths.
Struggling toward transformation,
moths burst into flame.
Throwing open all the doors and windows,
ripping off corporate masks,
overthrowing capital lies,
abolishing bankers' games.
Suddenly we are all visionaries,
rebirth in our hearts and brains,
reinventing our world.
What has never been seen before,
which way is the rain?

Billboard: Corporate Economy Collapsing

Corporate economy collapsing!
We don't need them;
survival means seizing our freedom!
We have nothing but each other.

COLUMBUS IN THE BAY OF PIGS

The Beginnings of Indigenous Resistance to the European Invasion of America

1

Yaní tainó, yaní tainó.
Let the Taino language be heard.
Yaní tainó, yaní tainó. Dayaní.
Goeíz nitaynó guajirós guacá!

A dark night, April seventeenth, nineteen-
sixty-one: while the U.S. Navy watches,
not far away, fourteen hundred exiles,
recruited in Miami by the CIA,
sail quietly toward the Bahía de Cochinos,
the Bay of Pigs, toward the palm-shaded sand
of Playa Girón, weapons bulging in every hand,
and in their crosshairs, the young
Cuban revolutionaries, for their sin
of overthrowing a brutal dictator
and their sin
of trying to break the stranglehold
of the all almighty dollar.

Imagine la arena de Playa Girón,
fina y blanca, que gira
el rincón
de la Bahía de Cochinos,
Cuba.

Imagine the sand of the beach called
Girón, fine and white, the big bend
that turns the corner of the Bay of Pigs,
Cuba.

Touch it. Take some in your fingertips.

Let it fall. You are touching
the blood of empire.

Tócala. Tómala en las puntillas. Déjala caer.
Está tocando la sangre de imperio.

A cloudless midday, May twentysixth,
fourteen-ninety-four, two years after his first
"voyage of discovery," the Italian Cristoforo
Columbo - Christopher Columbus - called
by the Spaniards Cristóbal Colón - approaches
the mouth of the Bay of Pigs. He is
on his second voyage to "the Indies."
He thinks he is off the coast of China,
and carries letters of state
from the king and queen of Spain
to the Great Emperor Khan.
He stands on the quarterdeck, squinting
at the shore, wondering
if Cuba is finally the mainland he seeks.
The sun is a searing disc
directly above his head. His troubled thoughts
turn back to Isabela, his colony on Haiti,
with half his men sick, the rest angry and bitter,
little gold collected, food supplies low,
the Indians strained and wary.

Yesterday's shore had been lined
with Indian villages, the ships
often surrounded by Taino-Arawaks in canoes
offering songs and gifts to their visitors
from "the sky," (not yet understanding
what it meant
to be subjects of a European king), but today
at the mouth of the Bay of Pigs
Columbus sees no village, the shore
is mangrove swamp, impenetrable.

Suddenly
glistening before them: a white

crescent of sand laced with palm groves.

Churning water: a great herd of beasts!
The Indians call them manatee,
but the seamen call them pigs.

The boats are lowered;
the rowers pull their oars; the hulls
glide through the waves, up onto the beach.
Columbus steps out; his foot sinks
softly into the sand of Playa Girón.

From his log book, these
are his very words:

"At the edge of the sea,
in a great grove of palms
that seemed to reach the sky,
there gushed forth two springs
of water, and when the tide
was on the ebb, the water
was so cold and so sweet
that no better could be found in the world.
No people appeared, but there were signs
of their presence in cut palms.
And we all
rested there on the grass by those springs
among the scent of the flowers
and the sweet singing
of little birds, and all was so gentle,
and the shade of the palms so grand and fair,
to see it all was a wonder!"

So Columbus gushed
over all he found in the Bay of Pigs,
as he did over so much in this New World.
But beneath the enthusiasm
was a dark side of Columbus,
an underside.

May twentysixth, fourteen-ninety-four;

April seventeenth, nineteen-sixty-one.

Sangre llena las huellas de Cristóbal Colón
en la arena pálida de Playa Girón;
blood fills the footprints of Cristóbal Colón
in the pale sand of Playa Girón.

He hadn't undertaken his "enterprise"
in the spirit of science,
but lusted for gold and power,
and sailed into the setting sun not just
to "discover" the Indies but
to conquer them.

That's the deal he wrangled
from the king and queen of Spain
three years before, that he,
though a commoner, a foreigner, would become
Governor and Viceroy of all
"islands and continents"
that he might "discover and acquire,"
as well as "Admiral of the Ocean Sea," and
be granted "the noble title of don."
And he would get to keep one tenth
of all "gold, silver, pearls, gems, spices,
and other merchandise" in these lands,
free of all taxes.

But none
of this Columbus was doing for himself
alone. No, he saw visions and portents
and had greater plans: he
had sworn to the Virgin Mary that if she
would guide him by this new route,
bypassing the Muslim blockade
of the road to the East, he would repay her,
within seven years,
by converting the Indies to the Christian Faith,
and by gathering its fabled wealth to pay
for a new crusade

to reconquer the Holy Land from the Infidels.
And the fall of Jerusalem
and recapture of the Holy Sepulchre of
Jesus by his troops, scheduled to occur about
the dawn of the year fifteen-hundred, Columbus
was certain, would be the signal for
the Second Coming.

Sangre llena las huellas de Cristóbal Colón
en la arena pálida de Playa Girón.

And when the Virgin Mary did - or so he
thought - guide Columbus across
the water, at the very first land he touched,
he began to repay her,
by kidnapping six Tainos:

"They interrogated us as if
we had come from heaven," he wrote,
"and cried out in loud voices
to the others, 'Come see the men from the sky.
Bring them food and drink.'
There came many of both sexes, every one
bringing something, giving thanks to God,
prostrating themselves on the earth, lifting up
their hands to heaven... I took by force six
of the Indians from the first island,
and intend to carry them to Spain in order
to learn our language and return, unless your
Highnesses should choose instead to have
them all transported to Spain, or held
captive on the island. These people are
very simple in matters of war... I could
conquer the whole of them with fifty men,
and govern them as I pleased... They are
all of good size and stature, straight-
limbed without exception, and handsomely
formed, with fine shapes and faces; their hair
short, coarse like a horse's tail, combed
toward the forehead except for a small

portion which they let hang down
behind, and never cut... Their eyes are very
large and beautiful... They quickly learn
such words as are spoken to them... They
are very clever and honest, display great
liberality, and will give whatever
they possess for a trifle or for nothing
at all... Whether there exists any such thing
as private property among them I have not
been able to ascertain... As they appear
to have no religion, I believe they would very
readily become Christians... They would make
good servants... They are fit to be ordered
about and made to work, to sow, and do
aught else that may be needed, and your
Majesties may build towns and teach
them to go clothed and adopt our customs...
Seeing some with little bits of gold
at their noses, I gathered by signs that by going
southward there would be found a king
with large vessels of gold in large quantities...
To sum up the great profits of this voyage, I am
able to promise, for a trifling assistance
from your Majesties, any quantity of
gold, drugs, cotton, mastic, aloe, and as many
slaves for maritime service as your
Majesties may stand in need of."

Those are the words of Christopher Columbus.

Yes, Columbus invented the slave trade
in the New World.

Sangre llena las huellas de Cristóbal Colón
en la arena pálida de Playa Girón.

2

Who were these Tainos?

Probably the friendliest
people in all the Americas: Taino means
"peaceful" or "good."

They lived in villages of round
palm-thatched caneys, some
with several thousand inhabitants.

The men and boys wore no clothes,
nor did the girls until their first menstruation,
then a small nagua, and after marriage
a woven cotton apron. They slept in net
hammocks. The women wore lightningbugs
in their hair.

Their main weapons
were cane spears with fishbone-tips.
They hunted the groundhog-like hutía
with trained little barkless dogs.
They used pet parrots to decoy wild ones,
then noosed their feet. They braved the sea
in cedar dugout canoes with square ends,
some large enough to carry eighty or more.
They tied a rope to the tail of the ramora-fish,
and, when the ramora attached itself
to another fish by its sucker mouth,
the fisherman would pull them both out.
The Tainos were great swimmers.

Their bread was cassava, baked
on a stone griddle. They kept a pepperpot soup
simmering at all times. They shaped clay
coils into pots, wove baskets from
biheo leaves. They mixed earth and ashes
into conuco mounds where they grew cassava;
near rivers they used ditch irrigation.
On hillsides they planted corn, five kernels
in each hole a pace apart. They grew yams,
beans, pepper, arrowroot, peanuts; kept
orchards of coconuts, papayas, mameys,

pears, annonas, guayabas, pineapples.

They had broad flat foreheads, from being
pressed between boards as infants. In their
pierced ears and noses, they wore
shell, bone, stone, and gold.
They painted their bodies
with symbols, the men preferring red,
the women yellow, white, and black.
They bathed daily, using digo root as soap.

To lock a house, they placed a stick
across the entrance, and no Taino would
think to pass.

Their only enemies were
the Caribs of the Lesser Antilles, who would
raid occasionally and take captives.
The Tainos never raided back.

Who were these Taino people?

At the hub of each village was a plaza,
a ceremonial center, with a temple housing
the village zemís. These were
effigies of stone, wood, shell, or gold, in which
resided messengers to the gods. Near
the temple was a court where they played
a ceremonial ball game in re-creation of a
heroic myth. Close by was the bohío, the
large rectilinear home of the cacique
and his - or her - extended family.
The cacique's job was the village welfare,
assigning the daily work routine, and
making sure everyone got a fair share. Two
of the six main caciques on Haiti when
Columbus arrived, were women.

The Tainos danced to areitos, songs of tribal
history, of the zemís, of love and mourning.
They danced revolving in circles,

with strings of rattling shells on their wrists
and ankles, waving palm fronds, to the sound
of hollow-log drums, shell timbrels, copper and
gold castanets. The bohuti-priests sang areitos
to cure the sick, to the drone of a maiohavan,
a wooden gong with a long neck, so resonant
it could be heard a half league away.

Who were these Taino people?

They believed there is an immortal
being in the sky whom none can see,
who has a mother but no beginning.
They called him Yocahu and his
mother Atabex. The zemís were
their messengers.

They believed that out of a cave called
Yoyovava on the isle of Haiti came
the sun and moon; from two other
nearby caves, Cacibayagua and Amayauba,
came the Taino people.

They believed that the ocean was formed
from the great flood that poured out
of the stolen calabash
that Dimivan dropped.

They believed that at death their souls
journeyed to the beautiful valley of
Coaybay, presided over by the cacique
Maquetaurié, where they remained
in pleasure forever.

They had a myth - an old story, remembered
in many areitos - of how once a great cacique
named Guamiquiná, who wore
clothes and a beard, came down
from the sky in a ship,
from a place called Turey,
bringing precious gifts and teaching

the Taino people many skills. Guamiquiná
could only stay a short while then
left, promising to return someday.

Was it any wonder then, when
Columbus appeared at these same shores,
the Tainos called him Guamiquiná,
expected him to stay only
a short while, and were shocked when
they realized that he didn't plan
to leave at all?

In the zemí-temple was a round wooden table,
on which they kept powdered cohaba-root:
the bohuti-priest would place some
on the head of a zemí, sniff the cohaba
through a branched cane, fall into a trance,
speak with the zemí, then return with a message
in an archaic tongue. The word cohaba
meant "to pray." It was through the cohaba
that the cacique Cacivaquel spoke
with the zemí Yiocavugama, who gave him,
decades prior, a prophesy of the arrival
of the Christians and a warning
of what they would do.
All the caciques knew this prophesy, but hadn't
the heart to tell their people.

Sangre llena las huellas de Cristóbal Colón
en la arena pálida de Playa Girón.

3

On his first voyage, two years before
he reached the Bay of Pigs, Columbus wrecked
his flagship Santa María on a reef
off Haiti-Bohío-Quisqueya, the cultural center
of the Taino world. He was rescued
from the reef

by the local chief, Guacanagarí.

Columbus stayed only long enough
to build a fort, then sailed
back to Spain on the Niña,
leaving thirty-nine men behind.

Returning ten months later, Columbus found
the settlement burned to the ground.

Guacanagarí had tried to protect the
Christians, but they'd abused the Taino
people until Caonabó,
"Golden House," cacique of the golden
mountains of Cibao, the most powerful
chief on Haiti, came down and
killed them all.

Caonabó was held in awe
by the Tainos. By blood half Carib,
the Tainos' only tribal enemies,
he had risen through sheer ability
to the top of the Taino world.
He shared power with his wife,
Anacaoná, "Golden Flower,"
renowned for wisdom, graciousness, and beauty.

Columbus knew
he'd have to settle the score
with Caonabó someday. But first business
was start a new settlement, "Isabela,"
gather gold, and discover the mainland.

So Columbus
left most of his men on Haiti
and sailed off once more,
to the Bay of Pigs and beyond, until
he was so certain
that Cuba was the mainland
that he made his entire crew sign an oath
that they would never say it was an island

(like the stubborn Indians insisted)
under penalty of having their tongues cut out.

On his return to Haiti,
he found the colony in disastrous straits.
Little gold had been collected, far from enough
to cover expenses, much less fulfill
his extravagant promises.

In desperation
he proposed to the king and queen
(as a temporary expedient of course,
until the gold mines begin to produce),
a plan to capture and sell
all the Carib Indians
on the grounds
that they were implacable cannibals
and fierce enemies of Spain's friends,
the Tainos.

But the king and queen balked,
as the first few Indians he'd sent quickly died.

Meanwhile, gangs of soldiers were roaming
Haiti, skirting only the province of Caonabó,
committing brutalities of every sort
against the Tainos, who suffered in silence until
one chief, Gua Tiguaná,
ambushed three Spaniards and killed them.

Columbus didn't hesitate:
by Spanish law, "rebels" could be enslaved;
besides,
Tainos were easier to catch than Caribs.
He sent his army to their village, rounded up
fifteen hundred men, women, and children,
chose five hundred fifty of the fittest,
boarded them on four ships, and sent them off
to the slave market in Seville;
the rest Columbus offered to the colonists
as personal slaves, his complements, no charge.

Two hundred died aboard ship,
and most of the rest soon after arrival.
Gua Tiguaná was condemned to death by arrows,
but chewed through his ropes
and escaped to the mountains,
where he organized resistance.

Columbus found him and attacked
with artillery, cavalry, infantry, and dogs.
In the end, Gua Tiguaná's people
made Columbus another few shiploads of slaves.

Yet he was only a subchief
to the great cacique Caonabó,
who had to be approached now,
but with more caution.

Columbus sent a delegation with gifts
to Caonabó, led
by the intrepid Lt. Ojeda, already famed
as the first to enforce Columbus' decree
to cut off the ears or nose of any Indian
stealing Spanish property.

In his village,
high in the mountains of Cibao, Ojeda
met Caonabó, who wore a crown "with wings
on its sides like a shield and golden eyes
as large as silver cups." Ojeda told him
that Columbus offered peace,
if only he would come down
to the settlement to talk. Caonabó, despite
everything, responded, "Yes,
if Guamiquiná wants peace,
I will make peace. I ask only one thing:
to be given
the Christians' church bell as a sign."
So they started down.

Stopping at a river bank, Ojeda held up a
set of manacles to Caonabó, and said,

"These are ceremonial bracelets,
worn only by kings on horseback:
Lord Columbus
has sent them for you to wear
on this great occasion."

So Caonabó became the first Indian
to ever ride
one of these magic creatures called horse.

Caonabó was tied to the saddle behind Ojeda,
the chains locked on his wrists and ankles;
Ojeda suddenly spurred the horse
across the river, away from the startled
Indian delegation, and hardly stopped until
they reached the settlement, where the greatest
chief of Haiti, instead of being given
the church bell, was thrown at Columbus'
feet, then chained on the porch
of Columbus' house
on the main plaza, for all to see.

The entire island,
except for the village of Guacanagarí,
rose in revolt,
but the Tainos' fishbone-tipped spears
were no match for cold steel,
so all the island was quickly conquered,
and Columbus, imitating Caesar in Gaul,
imposed tribute on the native people.

Sangre llena las huellas de Cristóbal Colón
en la arena pálida de Playa Girón.

Each Taino over fourteen years of age
in the region of Cibao
had to pay enough gold
to fill a hawk's bell measure
every three months, and in return
received a brass token
to wear about his neck as proof

of up-to-date payments. Caciques had to pay
a half calabash full of gold
every two months. The penalty
for nonpayment was amputation of the hands.

The gold the Tainos possessed
had been collected over many generations;
within a season Columbus had it all
and the only way the Tainos
could fill their quotas was
to dig it from the river banks. Soon
the streams were filled with whole families,
desperately trying to find enough in time.
They began to flee to the highest mountains
and remotest spots, leaving their crops
unplanted, and famine stalked the land.

But the Christians came after them.
When the Tainos caught a Spaniard now,
they melted gold and poured it down his throat.

Columbus kept the great cacique Caonabó
chained on his front porch for two years, then
put him on a ship for Spain;
he died at sea.

One by one all the chiefs of Haiti,
Guarionéx, Behechió, Mayobanéx, Gua Tiguaná,
Cotubanamá, Cayacoá, Higuanamá,
Caonabó's wife Anacaoná,
were tortured, hanged, impaled, burned
at the stake, except for Guacanagarí,
Columbus' one unwavering friend, and he
was banished by his own village, for
Columbus had not exempted even them
from the horrors of the tribute collectors, so
Guacanagarí, an outcast, died
a squalid death on some remote peak.

The Tainos could not understand
why the Christians wanted this gold.

One cacique of Haiti, Hatuey, fled
with his people to Cuba. When told that the
Christians had followed them, he took out
a basket of gold, and said, "Here
is the God of the Christians. They want
us to worship this God: that is why
they struggle with us and kill us. Let us dance
for this God. Who knows? It may please
the Christian God and then they will do us
no harm."

So he and his people danced
before the gold. Then Hatuey hurled
it into the middle of a river.

Not long after,
the Christians caught him
and tied him to a stake. A friar who knew
the Taino language, told Hatuey,
just before they touched the flames,
"If you become a Christian, even now,
you will go to Heaven instead of
to the eternal torment of Hell."

Hatuey asked the friar, "Do
all Christians go to Heaven?" The friar
said, "They do;" and Hatuey replied, "I
would prefer then to go to Hell."

Sangre llena las huellas de Cristóbal Colón
en la arena pálida de Playa Girón.

And so the island of Haiti-Bohío-Quisqueya,
which in Taino means,
Mountain-House-Of Which Nothing Is Greater,
a land thriving with millions
of people when Columbus arrived,
within a short time was almost
depopulated.

Most of the Taino men wound up as slaves

in the mines, most of the women slaves
in the fields, where thousands died
of exhaustion, disease, and hunger.
Those hiding in the mountains saw
that all was lost, and thousands jumped
from cliffs, hanged or stabbed themselves,
or drank cassava poison.

And the beautiful Taino language
became silence.

Most of the gold, the treasure
of the Taino nation,
was stowed on a fleet bound for Spain,
but Guabancéx, the zemí of hurricanes,
aroused a great wind and sucked the gold
to the ocean bottom, to mix
with the bones of Caonabó.

Faced with a labor shortage, the Christians
sent soldiers to the other islands, to capture
slaves for the mines and plantations
of Haiti, and to begin setting up plantations
and mines on those other islands too.

Sangre llena las huellas de Cristóbal Colón
en la arena pálida de Playa Girón.

This is the Taino language.

Datoá guariquén ayacavó datiáo.
Mother, come meet my friend.

Mayaní, guaguá areitó ocamá.
Quiet, my baby, listen to the song.

Caconá behiqué chug, darocoél.
Take this gift of medicine, grandfather.

Itá caoná.
I don't have any gold.

Guaibá cristianós anaquí kanaimá.
Let us get away from the Christian devils.

Baizá! Mayanimacamá!
No! Do not kill me!

Opiá dacá.
I am dead.

4

What sort of man was this Columbus?

The son of a weaver, he pretended
to descend from an ancient Roman Consul.

Who was this Columbus?

As an incentive to the sailors on his
first voyage, the king and queen had
offered a reward to the first man
to sight land, a reward of forty thousand
maravedis per year for life: a trifle
for a rich man, a fortune for a poor.

It was a common seaman named
Rodrigo de Triana who was the first
to actually sight and cry, "Land!" but
when they got back to Spain,
Admiral Columbus claimed
- and got -
the reward himself, for his story of having
seen some beckoning light
in the dark the night before, even though
he never actually cried, "Land!" while
the seaman Rodrigo got nothing.

Who was this man Columbus?

He had read the imaginary
Travels of Sir John Mandeville,

and taken it literally, so when he
finally did reach the continent, at
the Orinoco river, Venezuela, Columbus
made perhaps his greatest discovery:

"The philosophers of old have described
the world as spherical," he wrote, "and I
have no doubt this shape is true of the
hemisphere known to them. But all my
observations and calculations of this
newly discovered part of the world, and
in particular my discovery of a river far
mightier than any other known on earth,
able to pour fresh water several leagues
out to sea, lead me to believe that this part
of the earth is far more elevated than the rest,
both land and water, and reaches its peak
far inland under the equator. I believe
that here, at the highest place, will be found
the Terrestial Paradise, as described
in the Bible, inaccessible to mortal feet but
by divine permission. I believe the great
river I discovered is one of the four said
to flow from the fountain springing
from the foot of the Tree of Life,
feeding the oceans of the world...
I believe now the earth is not shaped round
as a sphere, but like a pear, or
a woman's breast, with the Earthly Paradise
on the nipple."

It was here in Venezuela, on the aureola
of Paradise, that Columbus planned to start
his first mainland colony, in order
to sail upstream to Eden, with divine
permission, and to harvest
the nearby pearl beds he'd discovered.

Who was this man Columbus?

The Tainos were not the only ones
with reason to hate the Governor:
a steady stream
of colonists returning to Spain
accused him of
abuse of authority, fiscal mismanagement,
withholding of salaries, embezzlement,
boundless personal ambition. Some rose
in the first colonial revolt in the New World,
in alliance with the Tainos,
led by Columbus' former footman and squire,
Francisco Roldán, whom he in his wisdom
had appointed Chief Justice.

Meanwhile almost all the Indian slaves
that Columbus sent to Spain soon died, until
finally the king and queen decided to
send the last few Indians alive in Spain
back to the Indies, along with
a royal investigator,
Commander Bobadilla, who sailed
into the harbor of Columbus' new capitol,
Santo Domingo, on August twenty-third,
the year fifteen-hundred. The first thing
he saw was three swaying bodies
on the gallows, "rebels"
hanged hours before; the prison held more
"rebels," scheduled for hanging next dawn.

Bobadilla declared Columbus deposed and
ordered him arrested.

But the soldiers who confronted Columbus
suddenly took fright, and none
of them was willing to place the chains
on the Admiral of the Ocean Sea,
until a man stepped forward who knew him
so well he had no fear of him: Espinoza,
Columbus' personal cook, took the
chains from the soldier and snapped them

on his master's wrists.

And so Columbus was sent back to Spain,
to face the mercy of the Crown, and
never fulfilled his vow to the Virgin Mary.

Even with him gone, the mold
had been cast, the conquest and slaughter
on the islands raged on: Haiti, Cuba,
Puerto Rico, Jamaica,
the Antilles, the Bahamas,
millions of Taino-Arawaks dead,
the entire nation murdered
from the face of the planet, and even then,
the infernos in the mines and plantations
blazed hardly diminished, Tainos
replaced by Caribs, by Aztecs and Mayas
from the mainland, and by slaves
from Africa.

It was only the slave trade with Europe
that the king and queen saw fit to ban.
"Rebels" could still be enslaved, but had to be
kept in the Indies. When a Spaniard
was granted land, he was also "granted "
all the Indians living on that land, as serfs:
this was the encomienda system
used to subdue all Spanish America.

Sangre llena las huellas de Cristóbal Colón
en la arena pálida de Playa Girón.

5

And so the Caribbean of today
was slowly formed. As the native
people changed into the present
mixed population, so the yoke
of Spain was replaced by North

American domination, yet the Caribbean
people still found themselves
impoverished and enslaved.

In Cuba, 1959, foreigners
owned and controlled
seventy-five percent of all arable land,
the police chief of Havana received
seven-hundred-thirty-thousand dollars per month
graft from the gambling casinos,
while the new native people, the campesinos,
did not eat regularly.

But now the people had more than
fishbone-tipped spears to fight back with.

October 1958
the revolutionary guerrillas
of the 26th of July Movement announce
Revolutionary Law One, turning
the land worked by renters, tenants,
and squatters over to those who work it.

December 1958:
the guerrillas descend
from the Sierra Maestra mountains
and fight their way toward the cities.

January 1st, 1959:
the puppet dictator flees; the streets
of every village and city fill with dancers.

May 1959:
expropriation and redistribution
of the largest rural estates,
mostly owned and controlled
by North Americans and other foreigners.

May 1960:
all foreign-owned sugar mills and
enterprises bought with stolen money

under the Batista dictatorship are now
declared property of the Cuban people.

October 13th, 1960:
all banks and 382 vital industrial enterprises
including sugar and rice mills,
textile factories, railroads,
and coffee roasting plants are now
declared property of the Cuban nation.

October 13th, 1960:
all urban tenants are now homeowners and
urban landlordism is hereby abolished.

Six days later, October 19th, 1960:
the U.S. of North America
declares a general embargo on Cuba.

January 1961:
the U.S. of North America forbids
its citizens to travel to Cuba.

January 1961:
the U.S. of North America
breaks diplomatic relations with Cuba.

A dark night,
April 17th, 1961, while
the U.S. Navy watches not far away,
fourteen hundred exiles, recruited
in Miami by the CIA, quietly approach
the mouth of the Bahía de Cochinos,
the Bay of Pigs, weapons bulging in every hand.
While on the beach on the fine white sand
of Playa Girón, a jeep drives up,
and two startled Revolutionary Militiamen
shine their headlights into the face
of the oncoming waves...

Toca la arena. Tómala en las puntillas.
Déjala caer. Está tocando

la sangre de imperio.

Touch the sand. Take some in your fingertips.
Let it fall. You are touching
the blood of empire.

May twentysixth, fourteen-ninety-four;
April seventeenth, nineteen-sixty-one:

Sangre llena las huellas de Cristóbal Colón
en la arena pálida de Playa Girón.

Datoá, guariquén ayacavó datiaó.
Mother, come meet my friend.

Mayaní, guaguá, areitó ocamá.
Quiet, my baby, listen to the song.

Caconá behiqué chug, darocoél.
Take this gift of medicine, grandfather.

Dayaní.
I will speak.
Goeíz nitaynó guajirós guacá.
The Taino people live!

Yaní tainó, yaní tainó.
Let the Taino language be heard.
Let the Taino language be heard.

Yaní tainó, yaní tainó. Dayaní.
Goeíz nitaynó guajirós guacá!

SCATTERED SHOWERS
heartsongs

I'M STILL ALIVE!

I'm still alive!
I never thought I'd live past twenty-five,
and now the seasons have changed
and changed many times since that year.
Gone are the tearless fears
gone the fearful tears,
and in their place this beautiful surprise
this gift this laughter this time free and clear
this raft of logs and hide
coasting down a gentle tide
past emerald ports rocked in symphonies of desire,
past storm-torn towers with windows spitting fire,
with only the current to trust as a guide
and only the wind and my heart to steer.

BUT ANYWAY WHAT'S IN A NAME?

And the Lord said to Noah,
"Build me an ark, and of every living thing
bring in two of each sort, male and female"
Then the waters prevailed and blotted
all that lived from the face of the earth
except those with Noah and his wife.
History does not record
how that little menagerie
whiled away the days but my guess is
Noah holed himself in the captain's cabin
and waited for another message from God
while it was his wife who kept the trip together
cleaning up animal shit.
Christian, Judaic and Muslim traditions
all recognize Noah as the Second Adam
our common father while the same traditions
do not even bother to record her name.

ALL THE UNSPOKEN

all the unspoken things hover between us
like ghosts between scaffolds . . .

UPTIGHT

You took my sorrow and borrowed my tomorrow,
and now that I want them back,
you say you lost them somewhere near Boston
down by some railroad tracks.
You say, "They just fell out the door."
But why were you lying on the car floor?
I tell you honey I can't walk without it;
but you say you don't want to talk about it:
You twist an earring of mother-of-pearl
and whisper sharply, "I'm just that kind of girl."
And now you stop me in the hall
and throw my toothbrush against the wall
and insist you have to know why.
You cry, "All couples go through a little estrangement
so why don't we just make a little arrangement?"
Well honey, cause I'm just not that kind of guy.

APPROACHING PARANOIA

Q: You know I trust you,
honey,
to act the same when we're together
and when you're alone.
But who is that who keeps hanging up
whenever I answer the phone?

A: Probably the FBI.

DOWNSTARES

my love is cruel like silk
and changing as the sky
she wants what I do not have to give
she gives what she knows I do not want
my eagerness makes her reluctant
she rolls through my fingers like mist,
she mocks me, she dreams secret dreams
until I no longer know the sweet sounds of night
nor guard the secrets of children

I am a starfish I peek from the mud
beneath a rock with small red pebble eyes.

I am cruel like the sky and changing as silk
I want what she does not have to give
I give what I know she does not want
her eagerness makes me reluctant
I roll through her fingers like fog, I mock her
I dream secret dreams
I am a distant red star

JAYS

All the robins are gone; today
jays hop about the walnut
tree in my back yard,
cry and shake their blueblack
crests; the nuts are
rotten with worms; still
an orange squirrel above
my head gnaws them, chatters a
complaint then throws them half-
eaten on the ground, as clouds
in blotches grey like soot
drift past a feeble
sun: my love is lost in
dreams; even as I hold your
hips you lie alongside waterfalls,
biting strangers' lips; and as for
me I see all others in the shadows
of your eyes, and that is
why I'd kiss you should I kiss
another's thigh
and different faces pass and fade
away behind my eyes as I
lie drifting in your
restless tide; but why
then does the solid ground
inside my chest
give way and I find myself in a
terrible void, plummeting
down, why do I
moan and sigh?
. . . for love only streams
from the heart not the dream . . .
a robin above me cried.

A CERTAIN MOOD

Days can climb tough when you're on your own,
nights can crash rough when home means alone
licked by the waves of the city's strange moans
and you're just not getting off no more
on sliding free to roam
with your body under water and your mind under wind,
gazing into eyes in the crowd,
floating down the street in a cloud.

They say, you got to find something to strive for
have drive for
if you don't start soon you'll never arrive, did
you think it was enough just being alive, kid?

You swore you'd never get wrecked in a role
it had to grip real, glide whole
you had to ride it with your spirit
let your soul unfold
but now all you feel is the wind and the cold
shuddering along the cracks of your dislocated bones.

There's your old camp buddy with his filthy rags
your tenth grade sweetheart with her
hot pants and icy stares, the short-change
artists with their breasts bare, the wage-
earners in torn underwear, the storm troopers
in their pancake masks, the store-owners in
their bullet-proof flags, and the false priests
in their foul airs and the insurance salesmen in
their electric chairs.

Looking for someone to ease
your brain, looking for something to heal the
pain, trying to let your
self be, trying to let your mind
see, feeling whatever you got to feel, waiting for

something to be revealed, a
leaf drifting near a fall, a brief
encounter in the hall, gazing into
eyes in the clouds, floating down the street like a
crowd.

LOVE HANDLES

River spirit touch me please
with lilies twisted about your knees
dank hair tangled with stormy skies
ocean brooding behind deep eyes

Moon rider you know what you done
you threw my colors out to bleach
in the bony stare of the sun
and now my soul's sulking alone
in a closet of limestone
a bass note out of reach
a dead bird on an empty beach

Hard lady stay out of my trees
my branches are trembling with too cruel a breeze
my shock absorbers are too shot
my brains are blue hot

Look honey I ain't afraid
but your touch is like a razor blade
and don't pull that steel pin
sticking out of my secret heart
or my grenade will blast your whims apart

Hey lover I take back what I said
I m sorry for the fleas I put in your bed
I'm sorry for the squirting flower I
hid inside your head
and for its sudden shower on your
thought of the hour I'm sorry
for what the thunder said

Love hands lets go get blessed
I know a place where we can slip
into a robe of darkness
blue lightning twisting round a fountain
bowl moon rising beside a mountain

HEARSAY

They say a man can't understand a woman
and I wouldn't disagree,
but then again they also say a man
can't understand another man
so that's why, you see,
I'm daring to be presumptuous and say
I thought I understood you yesterday.

WE WALKED ALONG

We walked along together,
my lover and I,
together watching the Spring sun
drift through a cloudless sky,
laughing at a wild yellow rose,
laughing at a distant train,
looking at each other
and laughing again,
we walked so close
it almost seemed we were one.

But there's a rule of the road
we thought we could go
without obeying:
people who get too close
are soon separating.

We both feel the tire treads
skid across our brains
and see death
bouncing toward us
in a pickup truck
across a colorless shadowless plain.

but somewhere beyond
the savaging tears
and chattering pain
we both also know
our roads might meet
in a sweet
comingtogetheragain

SOMETIMES I WISH

Sometimes I wish
you weren't really you
so I could see you
without feeling all the
pain we've been through
(there's such heavy dues
in loving)

But sometimes
suddenly you glow
dawn new
I got to hug you and whisper
"Love,
we've come through!"
and kiss away your every bruise
(there's such a well of renewal
in loving).

DREAM

She is talking
in her sleep. I
listen for a while but
it is very garbled.
"Lover," I finally
say, "you're talking in your
sleep . . ." The words
are difficult to
pronounce. I force
my eyes
half open just as
she says, "Lover, you're
talking in your sleep . . ."

ALL THE PEACHES

All the peaches were slightly bruised
but the price was right. I was
examining a flattened mud-brown spot about
the size of a nickel, when
some words blew by and
turned my eye to two women beside the cabbage and carrots,
one about fifteen, the other about forty-five.
From the tilt of their jaws and the
twist of their ears I felt
sure they were mother and daughter.
I thought I'd heard, in a
quiet tone like dark water,
"women are the keepers
of the mystic bowl
in which the soul is brewed"
But I wasn't sure.
To look at them
I would have guessed
the older was chatting to the younger now
about the lettuce or watercress.
The older moved with a comfortable sag,
dropping a celery bush
into a plastic bag;
the younger kept glancing
down a far aisle,
rubbed her knees together slightly
and bit her lower lip;
she looked as if she didn't quite fit
into her just-blooming womanness. I
slipped closer and leaned my head to
hear the older say to the younger,
with eyes like stained glass,
"women are the openers
of the magic door
through which the future
mind must pass,
the offerers

of the perfect spring
where the spirit must drink
to grow strong"
she placed three tomatoes on a scale then
went on,
"but that doesn't mean you
have to take that kind of shit from
that jerk, Ellen, stand . . . Ellen
are you listening?"
"I know I know" the
younger replied impatiently then
suddenly noticed me and blushed.
"All the peaches are slightly
bruised," I shrugged,
"but
the price is right."

I HEARD THE SONG

I heard the song of my death
calling to me
from a spiral just out there
but oh so close to me
and it sang
oooo ooo ooo oooo oooo
oooo ooo ooo oooo oooo
so soon I knew fear was nothing
and so I had nothing to fear

I heard the song of my life
calling to me
from a spiral inside here
oh so close to me
and it sang
oooo ooo ooo oooo oooo
oooo ooo ooo oooo oooo
so soon I knew fear was nothing
and so l had nothing to fear

THE WIND BLOWS

the wind blows your hat off
a one-eyed fish with a headlamp
stares at you through the porthole
I just stubbed my toe on a puddle
don't forget to zipper your fly

you fall in love with a pillow
I've got a chipmunk in my pocket
examining little pieces of stuff in the gutter
a redbrick building waves to us as we drive by

you spent the whole morning playing with your toes
hey they wont let you do that on the bus
why is that bird laughing
two supernova collide

poem for gary johnston
Africa rises from the foaming waves
I'll stay with you forever
the panhandlers pray for rain

feeding the children of paraguay
beetles don't recognize private property
because your pants are filled with wind
but there's so much pain

they exchange your head for an elephant's
you tickle a cop with a sunbeam
you are sent as ambassador to the eskimos
you make world war two not have happened
you do a little dance to this poem
they crown you with a birthday hat
you leap into a secret pond
a greeneyed frog dives through the front wall
riding the rising sun through a cloud of infinite sound

you blow a little kiss to god

ALMOST TO

1
B1ackberries tangle lazily
along the fence grey
and weathered to the grain.
Lapwings in the roses and
poinsettias by
the window. A cobweb
sparkles in the corner
of the sill; an ant
explores the dust;
droplets ramble down
the beaded glistening
pane. Early
morning, blue and pale, seeps
like milk through the leaves and
across pillow-strewn hair. Beneath
the comforter her foot
is barely brushing
mine. In the other
room baby stirs.

2
laughing girl
when you dance around
your flowery dress whirls
and petals drift to the ground.
Did you tie that blue ribbon
around your cat's tail?
What did your grammy
send you in the mail?
Where do you and your friends set sail
when you float in your ship of dreams?
Browneyed girl who lives in the back
you dance like a silvery stream.

TIMES 2

1
There are times I've looked
for love but could find only
sex, times I've looked for
sex but could find only
love, times I've
looked for anything or
nothing but couldn't find
it, time's
a string of colored beads,
sex a clasp
and love's a locket.

2
one way to pass
through this reality
is with love for all things
equally. To
love a thing,
share with it
care for it with compassion
accept the limits of its flesh, the
burdens of its mind
seeing all things in it including
yourself. Begin
slowly. Choose one thing and
love it. Then, as need be and
if time allows, add
another.

TRULY

I love you like
I love to look at things
I can't afford to buy,
I love you like
I love to talk to people who don't reply,
like a forest loves fires,
a jury loves liars,
like a miser loves a penny in each eye,
I love you so much I
could cry...

I love you like a
seagull loves to rub against the sky,
like a convict loves his dope,
a worker loves his hope,
a mountain loves a cold singing stream,
a yogi loves a cosmic dream,
I love you so much I could scream . . .

SPRING RITUAL

narrative poems & ballads

A CHANCE ENCOUNTER

I was walking down the shadows under a moonless sky,
when I saw two men in the alley - I couldn't believe my eyes:
one looked like Martin Luther King,
with suffering etched in his brow,
the other I could have sworn was Ronald Reagan,
shuffling a deck of cards under his smile.

Reagan slipped off his watch and rings and tossed them on the ground,
whipped out a wad of C-notes and threw them down.
"It's all yours, one draw of the deck." He flashed a terrible grin.
Martin replied, "Raise the stakes: I'll leave forever if you win
but if my card's high you leave and never come back again."

Martin crossed his arms one way then the other.
Reagan hunched his shoulders with a little shudder,
and muttered, "You draw first."
Martin's eyes were shining, his lips pursed;
his craggy fingers turned the card,
an ace of hearts faced the light.
Reagan swallowed hard, drew his cape up tight,
reached slowly toward the deck, smirking like a stock broker,
when suddenly Martin grabbed his wrist: "I saw you palm that Joker!"

Indeed Reagan clutched a Joker -
where it came from I didn't see.
"Don't ever," Reagan gasped, "ever touch me!"
and lunged at Martin savagely.
Martin deftly sidestepped
and Reagan crashed into the garbage cans,
then staggered to his feet,
the Joker still trembling in his hand.
He threw the Joker on top of the stake.
raised one finger into the air.
Three shots rang suddenly out.
They seemed to come from nowhere.

Blood dripped down Martin's ear,

blood dripped down his side.
Martin raised both arms.
"I'll be back someday," he cried,
and collapsed into my tears.
Reagan picked up the cards and bills and watch and ring,
brushed off his suit, slipped into the shadows
and disappeared.

So when you're walking down the shadows, under a moonless sky,
when you see two men in an alley - you better trust your eyes.
And when you're dealing with a Joker,
aces don't enforce the laws of chance;
and when you're dueling with a Gambler,
keep your eyes on both his hands.

STRICTLY CONSTITUTIONAL

Went to a party on the courthouse stairs:
you should have heard that bad band wail:
the sax was smoking down the drummer's tail
while the guitar melted the locks on the jail

the night the dockets caught fire
and we boogied from darkness to dawn
you should have been there with us carrying on
the night the stocks caught fire

Harry said to Mary, "Look here comes the heat
better stash your stash and get your shoes on your feet"
Mary said to Harry, "Lover don't be dismayed
it's only the comrades from the Emma Goldman Brigade"

the night the dockets caught fire

Firetrucks arrived like a flock of screech owls
but they just couldn't breech our surging wall
when we locked arms and howled,
you should have seen the chief,
his face hanging like a side of beef
and his eyes rolling wild, crying,
"Think about the governor, consider the neighbors"
as we carried out the deeds, the police files
and the incorporation papers

the night the stocks caught fire

Hooting and stomping like unchained slaves
round those prancing embers and those sky-licking flames
when the music suddenly stopped and we turned and saw
a shadow standing by the courthouse door,
draped in a hood and long black robe,
yelling, "Stop in the Name of the Holy Ghost!"

But Ghost,
who was leaning against a broken lamp post,
just laughed, fingered His Holy Nose

and went right back to His Marshmallow Roast

the night the dockets caught fire
and we boogied from darkness to dawn
you should have been there with us carrying on
the night the stocks caught fire

A pale moon still hovered in the west
the east was singed with dawn
we hung upon each others' necks
swaying back and forth
a pigeon settled on the flagpole mast
the band jammed slow
thin smoke swirled through the waking streets
ashes started to blow

FARMWORKERS SONG

[the California fields in 1974]

Downtown steel & glass,
office suite on the 21st floor,
pasty necks on top of ties,
silver cufflinks, manicured hands,
those are the "farmers" of our land:
Bank of America, Tenneco, Safeway,
Union Oil, Southern Pacific Railway,
financiers profiteering seed to supermarket,
controlling 80% of our farmable land.

And doing all the real work
down there in the sun-scorched rows,
backs cracking,
hardly able to straighten
after a day with the short-handled hoe,
are the "hired hands,"
whole families, children too,
sometimes ten, twelve hours a day,
following the harvest farm to farm.

Pesticide cloud blows in your face,
arm caught in a harvesting machine.
Foreman says: "You got 30 plants
to prune every hour. If you don't,
hit the road, tell your complaints
to the white line. And take off
your hat when you see the boss."

Then as soon as the crops are in
or as soon as you're hurt & can't
work any more: "Get lost."

And the pay so low,
at the end of the week
sometimes everything you earned
goes right back to the boss
for what you ate from his price-gauging store
& for sleeping in his chicken coop,

so it's hard to get even a few days ahead
by the time he lays you off.
Not even eligible for unemployment.

And you've got no legal right
to a union
to fight to better your situation,
because grower payoffs
got farmworkers excluded from the labor laws.

So years ago
the California grape-workers
began to organize themselves into
the United Farmworkers Union,
UFW,
stood together in Delano
& declared
they'd work no more under slave conditions.

And after ten bitter years of picket, march,
boycott & petition,
won a few contracts & a few recognitions.

And farmworkers from Washington State
to Florida caught fire & began to organize.

So the growers & financiers turned
to President Richard Nixon,
who gladly conspired with them
to wreck the union
before it swept across the nation.
For they shared a great fear
of seeing workers
democratically organized.

They agreed on an old
tried and true idea,
bring in the labor racketeers:
as soon as each contract expired,
they'd set up a phony union in place of the UFW,
fronted by the Teamsters,

who were controlled by gangsters at that time,
no elections,
kick ass,
& everyone who refuses to join gets fired.

Strike! Strike! 5 counties, 63 farms,
7000 workers ranch after ranch
thousands of black eagles
soaring on red flags.

But the growers owned the courts & politicians,
so the judges scribbled injunctions forbidding pickets,
the deputies cracked skulls & packed the jails;
the coyotes trucked in armies of scabs,
& workers' lifetime savings were drained
for doctors, fines & bails.
Teamster-salaried goons stalked the roads
with tire-irons, leather straps,
grape-stakes, chains & knives;
& teams of growers with high-powered rifles
prowled the countryside.

Hundreds hospitalized, thousands jailed.

Alicia Uribe, blinded, brass knuckle, right eye.
Nagi Daifullah, massive brain hemorrhage, died.
Juan de la Cruz, 66, bullet through the heart on a picket line.

The United Farmworkers Union almost destroyed.

And that's where things stood
if you were a farmworker
in the USA in 1974.

In the following years, the Teamsters left farm organizing
and became a better union.
But beyond that, things haven't changed much
for farmworkers since then until today.
For the most part, farmworkers remain
exploited and unorganized.

So next time you sit down to a meal,
think of the hands in the fields
that put some work into that food for you,
& help them defend themselves
against police-state, labor racketeers
& monopoly financiers.

Back in 1974 we boycotted grapes, head lettuce
and any brand of wine made in Modesto,
because it was all scab Gallo wine;
when we could, we joined a march & a picket line,
for we knew it was our struggle too.

And keep your ears pealed
for shots in the fields;
get ready to help if you hear the call.
We're all lost if we don't stick together.

It's the farmworkers who feed us all.

TYRONE

Emeryville 1973, the night after Halloween.
Tyrone Guyton was walking home.
He was just fourteen.

Not tall for his age and with a young face,
eyes so open and gullible,
he liked to study after school,
spend time with his family,
never been in any trouble.

Three whitemen in business suits
drifted by in a long sedan.
"Ain't that strange," one muttered,
"a black boy starting up a white chevy van."

Ty cruised slowly down the ave
then saw them in the glass;
he cut down 33rd Street,
they suddenly gated on his tail,

rammed his bumper hard,
he lost control, jumped the curb,
crashed into a wall.

Tyrone scrambled out the door,
saw revolvers waved,
tried to make a break
felt a blazing flash
fell flat on his face.

Those unmarked cops claimed he had a gun
but no gun was ever found;
the only two witnesses said
they handcuffed Ty behind his back
then blasted him through the back of his head
while he was lying bleeding on the ground.

Still, it didn't take that judge and grand jury
long to decide

it wasn't murder but justifiable homicide:
those cops were just doing their job,
protecting private property
from those who haven't got any,
and trying to keep the people scared.

Now, this town's full of kids
hanging out on the street:
the big cars are passing, the money flashing,
daddy needs new pants, mama's out of work,
and even when you got a job
there's just enough to eat;
and the stores are flaunting clothes and food,
rats scratching behind the walls of the apartments,
and you know
its the banks and finance companies who really own
most of those shiny cars,
and when the people can't pay
they take them away
and sell them over and over again
and they keep the cops and courts
as their accounting department.

Every fourteen-year-old knows
that to break the law
is to strike back
at those who dictate the laws.

So the cops keep on killing
the grand juries keep acquitting
and the kids keep filling
up the jails and the morgues.

And it's never going to stop
until we lock
those hired guns and licensed crooks in jail
and open the jails to release our own.

Now and here's a place to start:
JUSTICE FOR TYRONE

THE SAN FRANCISCO GENERAL STRIKE

In 1934 the longshoremen of San Francisco
were grossing about ten dollars weekly pay;
the bosses wrung your sweat
twenty-four to thirty-six hours in a single shift,
then they'd dump you out of work
for three or four days.
You had to
leave your loves alone
in the dawnless hours,
never knowing when you'd be back home:
it was, shape up at the dock
hoping they'd finger you from the pack
while the chill fog sliced down your back
and burned like acid into your bones.

The shipping bosses
wouldn't even talk to the maritime unions,
so thirty-five thousand up and down the coast
voted strike;
with mass pickets in every port
from San Diego to Bellingham and Seattle,
we plugged the Pacific basin uptight.

In the city of Francisco, the gentle saint
who spoke to beasts and birds
of love for all the wonders of creation,
the Employers Industrial Association
was backroom king of the hills,

and enforced their regal will
with gangs of dogs and packs of sharks:
when they nodded the newspapers snapped in unison,
when they whistled the police growled and barked.

They ordered their troops to the Embarcadero:
"Don't drag your tails back here till that strike's dead!"
On the morning of July 3rd, 1934,
the steel doors
of Pier 38

clanged open
and a scab convoy roared out,
eight squadcars bristling with guns
at their head.

Thousands of us were massed and ready,
and when we saw them we surged and stopped them cold;
from behind us they attacked on horseback,
bouncing clubs off skulls and making brains unfold:
we dragged them off their nags
and made them a little less bold.
Then foot squadrons charged tossing teargas bombs;
we were forced to meet force with force:
an old brick will do just fine;
we had two-by-fours stapled to our picket signs;
anything we could find and lift
we hurled at them:
the Embarcadero was a scramble of fighting men.

For two hot days the battle rampaged;
workers swelled our lines from every union in town;
the Employers Association
and the Chamber of Commerce screamed:
"This is a communist insurrection
and must be put down!"

Then they upped the ante on us:
vomit gas knocked us in the gutter by scores;
shotgun pellets sprayed into our arms and faces,
we couldn't hold our places;
we carried hundreds off bleeding to the emergency wards;
Nick Bordoise and Harry Sperry
we carried off bleeding to the morgue.

Forty-seven hundred National Guards stormed the waterfront
under orders from Governor Stooge,
and sealed it off with bayonets,
barbed wire, machinegun nests,
and commands to shoot to kill
anyone who dared

try to stop the high-paid scabs
from unloading the stolen gold
from the holds of their pirate ships.

All across the city
livingrooms and union halls
rumbled with the same alarmed thought:
if the bosses get away with this
all the unions will be lost.

Painters Local 1158
sent out the call for a general sympathetic strike;
unions all over the city began to vote
while the Chairman of the Board of the AFL
yelled he forbade it
and most of the Central Labor Council resisted.

But the real union's not the bureaucracy's playpenned child
but the living collective of the rank-and-file,
and we can take direct power
any time we choose:
on the morning of July 15th, 1934,
the stores were silent,
the factories were locked,
the streetcars were dead,
the highways were blocked:
one hundred thirty thousand out and for four days
nothing moved in the city
without permission of the strike committee.

Except the vigilante packs
who skulked around like pier rats hunting meat,
suddenly appearing at union halls
and socialist periodicals,
clubbing everyone they saw
and smashing everything they could reach
under the smiling-eyed escort of the police
who waited outside till the plainclothes boys
fled down some back street,
then swaggered in

and busted all
of us for resisting being beat.

"Now," some shouted, "End it now,
before more are dead
and all San Francisco's under martial law."

Others cried, "Spread it! If the bosses
get away with this here
they'll try it in a thousand other places too.
We can win by shutting down all America
if we need to!"

As the Central Labor Council struggled over the course,
Oakland and Portland voted general strike in our support.
But in a close vote the Council chose
to end the strike
and see how the bosses would requite.
If they didn't change their tune
we'd go out again
real soon.

But now the Employers Association wasn't strutting so tough;
four days of workers' solidarity, they decided,
was taste enough;
they sent their suit-and-tie boys to the maritime unions
with the message that
they'd like to get together (at your convenience of course)
for a little friendly chat.

Soon all maritime workers had won union recognition.
Longshoremen had a thirty hour week and a six hour day,
a democratic rotary hiring system
and time and a half overtime pay.

All during the strike and after,
the bosses' spokesmen
and their newsmen doubles
lashed out again and again
that communists were causing and leading
all the trouble.

And I wouldn't deny
some of the guys'
blood was running pretty red those days.
But how could it be any other way?
Socialists have pounded the lines
in every big America strike
since
wage-slavery's shackles first clanked
on American workers' ankles.

And socialists will be there in every big strike
until monopoly's lock is cracked,
their wageslave train de-tracked,
and liberated workers begin to drive
America's economy
for our equal needs, democratically,
just like it always should have been,
cause social justice means real freedom for working people
and socialists are just workers fighting to win.

SPRING RITUAL

[Since ancient times May Day has been a festival of rebirth, the start of the "maiden" month; in 1889 it was also declared International Workers Day, in memory of certain events which took place in the USA three years before.]

May the buds open to the joyful sun today,
may the grass and the children grow and be strong,
may the stars and planets harmonize this Spring day,
may all the lovers roll in the hay,
may this uncut jewel be renewed,
may we discover ourselves as flames in a great transforming fire,
may the dancing branches round our maypoles whirl the flames higher,
may we shed our useless winter skin, step forth whole again,
unsold again this May day.

But may we first remember our wintry dead before
we let our Spring revelry totally sweep us away.

Depression hit hard in 1873,
just eight years after the American Civil War,
hunger prowled sullen through the countryside
North and South, jobless mulled the restless city streets,
while in the factories life was spit-cheap
and workers' blood greased the smoking lathes,
sweating ten to eighteen hours a day
for starvation pay six days a week.

Strike Strike
in the coal fields where barons ruled with iron whips and chilling fire,
they crushed the strike and hung twenty miners, Molly Maguires.
Then the railroads erupted coast to coast,
engines burned, tracks overturned.
State militias sided with the strikers,
farmers poured out of the hills bringing food,
general strikes in Chicago and St. Louis,
while in Pittsburgh workers took the city and for five days in

July 1877
a flaring sun and a wide-eyed moon
watched down on what they called The Pittsburgh Commune.
But the president of national monopoly protection
called out the US Army and Marines "to prevent national insurrection,"
1000 jailed, 600 cut down with slashing lead,
and before the blood trains flowed again
over one hundred workers were laid out dead.

So for year after mutilated depression year
poverty and fear
remained American workers' daily bread.

But slowly in shadow workers started to organize again,
roots spread in the fertile soil
and sprouts pushed up to the light of day
and grew into strong organizations:
The Knights of Labor, The American Federation,
The International Working People's Association.

The Knights were by far the largest and
called on all workers skilled and unskilled
of all races to unite into their One Big Union and cure
the bosses' blight of guns and wealth,
abolish wage-slavery and transform this land
into a workers' "Cooperative Commonwealth."
Workers were angry, a new strike wave swirled,
in 1885 the Knights rocketed to five times the size
of the AFL, 750,000 members,
the largest workers' organization in the world.

The skilled-worker-only white-male-only AFL, on the other foot,
with 150,000 members, strived only for bread and a little butter,
and was the first union federation in America
<u>not</u> to challenge to boss system's slavish roots.

The 7,000-member International Working People's Association
was an organization of social justice activists,
with the same goal as the Knights,

“a free society based on cooperative production,”
but wanted to go faster and further.

Then the call rang out
through Eight-Hour Leagues
for a national strike on the first of May 1886
to give all American workers an eight-hour day,
and they'd take it (thank you boss) with no loss in pay.

From the brutal New York factories
through the feudal stockyards of Chicago
to the cruel docks of San Francisco Bay,
workers caught “the eight-hour madness”
and organized with epidemic fever
toward that joyful and perilous day.

The newspapers pumped out by the bosses
screeched for a police transfusion,
claiming that May first wasn’t really the date
for the 8-hour day, but
for a workers' uprising and socialist revolution.

And on May Day...
NATIONAL STRIKE
200,000 out around the country, 340,000 parading:
The Knights of Labor, The American Federation,
The International Working People's Association!

That first day passed in jubilation and peace...
which didn't soothe the indigestion of the bosses
or satisfy the hungry clubs of their police.

But when on the third day the strike began to even grow and
spread,
they kicked their cops out of bed
and in Chicago at McCormick Harvester they attacked:
six workers fell with bullets in the back.

Next evening a protest meeting
was held in the chill drizzle in Chicago’s Haymarket Square.
The police were there

and marched in with guns and clubs
demanding the workers disperse.

Suddenly a bomb ripped the cops' air
thrown from no one knows where.
Through the fiery cloud
the cops fired wildly into the crowd.

In the following days,
a reign of police terror flashed everywhere across the country,
smashing the strike in every city and town;
thousands beaten, hundreds jailed.
In Chicago at least twenty-eight workers killed by police;
Knight leaders in four cities charged with conspiracy.

In the months that followed
seven strike leaders were framed in show-trials.
Despite no evidence against them,
five were sentenced to death:
Parsons, Spies, Fischer, Engel and Lingg.
Albert Parsons was a Knight and a leader of the Eight-Hour League,
all five were members of the International Working People's Association.

Parsons, Spies, Fischer, Engel were hanged,
while Lingg only escaped the noose by taking his own life
the night before.

The police and legal attacks left the Knights of Labor shattered beyond repair;
the International no longer existed, blasted into boiling air.

But the powers-that-be just harmed a few loose hairs
of the American Federation of Labor.
Instead, they terrified and tamed the AFL bureaucracy.
So since that time the Federation has been running scared, and has played the role of Loyal Opposition,
never again a serious threat to Corporate rule

May we remember our wintry dead on this May Spring day:

1886 May Day National Strike: 33 workers dead
1887 sugar fieldworkers strike: 40 workers dead
1892 steel strike: 10 workers dead
1892 silver miners strike: 25 workers dead
1894 railroad strike: 25 workers dead
1905 teamsters strike: 20 workers dead
1909 garment workers strike: 10 workers dead
1913 copper strike: 73 workers dead

and the reign of terror grinds on...

1914 coal strike: 34 workers dead
1919 steel strike: 22 workers dead
1922 sharecroppers union drive: 105 workers dead
1934-5-6 strike wave: 88 workers dead
1937 steel strike: 10 more workers dead

and the reign of terror writhes on...

Parsons framed and executed,
Spies framed and executed,
Fisher, Engel, Lingg framed and executed,
Joe Hill framed and executed,
Frank Little, Wesley Everest executed,
Vanzetti, Sacco, Rosenburgs,
Juan de la Cruz, Malcolm,
Martin executed while helping lead a garbage strike,
Fred Hampton, George Jackson,
workingpeople dead workers dead workingpeople
dead workers dead more workingpeople dead

and the reign of terror groans on...

MAY THE AMERICAN WINTER END
MAY THE RAIN OF POLICE TERROR END
MAY THE WINDS OF GOVERNMENT TERROR END
MAY THE SLEET OF CORPORATE TERROR END

may the buds open to the joyful sun,
may we step forth renewed on this day once again,
may the working people of the world come together today,

may we turn a corner in our lives and in our history,
may we throw off our oppressions,
resolve our pain,
hug the children, touch each other again and again,
may we be totally alive today,
say things to each other we've never said before today,
may we love each other's race,
glimpse a planet harmonized in eternally alive space,
may our collective spirit rise round the world
and help set our collective body free,
may energy return to the people,
new life spring forth from the people this day,
may all lovers roll in the hay,
may this uncut jewel be renewed,
may the land return to the people,
the tools return to the people,
may the power return to the people this May day,
may we celebrate our bodies joy-joined in creation,
re-creation, preservation of this same conscious spark-in-flesh
that was our great-grandparents since the first rocks began to dance
and will be our great-grandchildren until energy never ends,
you the mother of the world, you the father of creation,
channels in an infinite living stream,
may we glimpse beyond the frosted seas of death
and wake from bad dreaming,
may all wounded flesh and hearts heal,
may the last hungry child be fed and kissed
and stop screaming,
may this uncut jewel be renewed,
may we discover ourselves as flames in a great transforming fire,
may the dancing branches round our maypoles whirl the flames higher,
may we step forth whole again unsold again this May Day.

HOMAGE TO GONZALO GUERRERO

In the year 8 Water,
the 11th tun in a 2 Ahau katún,
in the calendar of Castile the year 1511,
a small boat carrying seventeen shipwrecked
Spaniards washes up on the northern coast of
Lúumil Cutz U Lúumil Ceh,
the Land of Pheasant and Deer,
called by the Castillians, Yucatán.

These are the first Europeans to walk
in the land of the Maya, the Mayab.

Six tuns pass.
By the Maya year 1 Storm,
1517,
only two of the Europeans are still alive.
One, Gonzalo Guerrero, known as Warrior,
a seaman from Palos,
is now married to the daughter of
Ah Nachan Can, the Halach Uinic,
governor of the province of Chetumal.
Guerrero has become a Nacom, a lord of the
Serpent order.
The other shipwrecked Spaniard,
Jeronimo de Aguilar, known as Eagle,
has become a masehual, a common worker
attached to the lord of a small town near Chab Le.

Then in that same year 1 Storm,
1517,
three ships in search of slaves
appear off the coastal city Ecab.
From their decks the Spaniards can see
pyramids in the distance. They call the city
"Great Cairo," and think themselves
the first Europeans to reach this land.
Ten huge Maya canoes with sails,
almost as long as the ships,

forty men in each, come out to meet them,
and invite them to shore.
The Spaniards wonder why
the Mayas show no surprise or fear of them.
The next day on land the group of Mayas escort
them toward Ecab, when suddenly
a band of warriors attacks, wounding thirteen
Spaniards and driving them back
to the boats. Unknown to
the Spaniards, among the Mayas
is Guerrero, the man Warrior.

The next year, another Spanish fleet returns
for revenge, but like the first,
they are routed and flee.

Two more tuns pass.
Then, in the Maya year 3 Water,
1519,
called 1 Reed by the Aztec count,
Captain Hernán Cortés
leads a fleet of eleven ships, 110 sailors, 553 soldiers
and plenty of ammunition,
toward the great Aztec city México-Tenochtitlán,
which they have heard glistens with gold.
Stopping at the island of Cozumel off Yucatan,
Cortés learns that on the mainland
two Spaniards are living with the Mayas.
He summons them,
sending strings of green beads as ransom.

Aguilar quickly reports to Cortés.
But Guerrero refuses, replying,
"I am married, have three children,
I am a chief to my people
and captain in time of war... My face
is tattooed, my ears pierced... Give those
green beads to my beautiful children, and I will say
it is a present from my brother countrymen."

Cortés seethes and
exclaims, "I wish I could get my hands on him;"
sends Aguilar back to Guerrero to cajole him.
Guerrero's wife, having heard enough, cuts in,
"Stop trying to seduce my husband, you slave!
Go away, speak to us no more."

So Aguilar returns to Cortés
and becomes his interpreter.
Guerrero chooses
to remain a Maya.

The next attacks on the Mayab
begin in the year 11 Jaguar, 1527.

But the Mayas,
advised by the Nacom Guerrero, lord
of the Serpent order,
know how to deal with the aggressors.
Mayan pits cripple Spanish horses,
barricades stop them on approaches to towns,
the invaders' food supplies are cut off.
The Mayas fight a guerrilla war, leaving empty towns
and hollow victories.

It took the Spaniards only
two years to defeat the mighty Aztecs,
only months to topple vast Peru, but
after a decade of war Yucatan is still Mayan.

Gonzalo Guerrero, Warrior,
the first European to marry into
Native culture, to make this
his children's homeland, their people
his people, to defend them
in undying opposition to European
rape and plunder.

Guerrero, Warrior,
I see you in the bushes by the river's edge
with a thousand comrades.

You are distinguished from them only
by your beard.
Your skin is tattooed into a book of glyphs,
painted black and red;
massive jade rings are in your earlobes,
a jewel embedded in your left nostril,
your long hair in four plaits coiled around your neck.
A jaguar skin hangs from your shoulders,
your head crowned with a great
fan of quetzal plumes, radiant green;
tucked into the belt of your breech-clout
is a dagger and a club.
In one hand is a small round shield,
in the other you clutch a thick trident
with three blades of sharpened shell.

Four Spanish ships in the channel lower boats
and their army quietly rows toward shore.
As they begin to disembark the air
is suddenly shattered with the throb of drums;
conch-shell trumpets wail, whistles shriek.
A storm of stones and arrows darkens the sky.
Out of nowhere your force leaps upon them
in hand-to hand combat.
You shout and slash, Gonzalo,
with your trident axe, the razor-sharp shells
tearing at their mark,
your quetzal plumes shaking and shining.

As you fall, a great serpent watches and
an iridescent green bird
flies wildly across the sun.

Nacom Guerrero, Warrior,
dead in battle by the Ulúa river, Honduras,
in the year 7 Jaguar, 1536,
a Spanish bullet in your head.
We honor you.

BALADA DEL RIO SUMPUL

[El Salvador in the early 1980s.]

...and now you ask me why
don't we turn back?
I ask you back,
don't you hear the weeping fields and mourning waves?

On the south bank of a meandering river
in the deep Salvadorian jungle,
the village of Las Aradas, The Plowed Fields,
communal shantytown of cardboard and mud
haven of collective survival
hidden community of fifteen hundred
women and men, children and elders
across the Sumpul river from Honduras
refugees from the terror
of the ruling military junta

Before dawn, May 14, 1980
troops of the junta
joined by the paramilitary fascist
ORDEN (blackshirts, white skull-&-crossbones insignia)
quietly semicircle Las Aradas . . .

we were out seeding when bullets sprayed and splattered
dropping our hoes we dove for our rifles
children were screaming and animals falling
fistfulls of lead tore through mud walls
rooftops were burning and tumbling around us
militia stood bravely drenching with fire
slowly we backed into the arms of the Sumpul
to cross as we'd planned to the wilds of Honduras
but out of the brush stepped the Honduran army
blocking our way . . .

...Y ya me preguntas,
"¿Por que no nos volvemos?"
Te repongo,
"¿No puedes entender los campos llorandos y las ondas lamentandas?

when three hundred are left to vultures on a sunny morning
and twelve thousand in the past year disappear
to unmarked graves?"
Te digo las opciones:
persistimos como guerrilleros
ó nos doblegamos en cavernas colonizadas.
Uno u otro:
nos morimos como esclavas
ó derribamos la junta
y arrojamos sus huesos en cruz de latón
a sus patrones norteaméricanos,
al fascista General Haig, al jefe Rockefeller,
y al dictador Presidente Reagan.

...And now you ask me why
don't we turn back?
I ask you back,
"Don't you hear the weeping fields and mourning waves,
cuando abandaron trés cientos para los buitres
por un amenecer soleado
y desaparacen doce miles por sepulcros sin marcas
por el año pasado?"
I tell you, our only choice
is to fight on as guerrillas
or grovel in colonized caves,
die as slaves or tear down the junta
and toss their brass crossbones
back to their North American masters,
dictator Reagan, boss Rockefeller,
and fascist general Haig.

EARLY WARNINGS

CHANGE/TEARS

Cosmogony: Change

TURN BACK ANCIENT RAVENOUS SOUL
mouth stuffed eternal striving/strife
screaming child afraid of hunger age loneliness
400 billion cells newborn already dying
afraid to die
liberation energy
to 400 billion new cells transformed:
in the blood a dying docile race
afraid that life is death is death is life is death
suffocating mother to son to mother to son to mother
to the thousandth generation and why climb the stair...?

not
to wonder
as we rest our crumpled bodies on our crooked staffs
and sigh
why on that first orgasmic day
we did not dive back into the holy fires and die.

But what is more ultimate human
they say
than to strive (for but not for something)
is
is not
both is/is not
neither is/is not :
none of those.
Mantra of the chanting winds
anti-matter particle swirling irresistible near
his most arbitrary of all simultaneous worlds
400 billion years in every cell
memory of swamp spore
the race Subuti the race
& just to keep things going
our own kind...?

400 billion past and future
lightyears darkly through a prism
and will we make it...?
what is there to...?

Seasons break turn us about
drive us to wander to yearn
tumbleweed blow and shooting star
somewhere to somewhere
so quickly old
before birth (so many past lives)
just to watch the new supplant us before we have begun
so many rooms so many open doors
The world grows young with us or old and bitter
sibyl hermaphrodite
spirit barefoot dancing in that first swirl of energy
crystallizing into matter for an instant
flying apart shimmering fragments in space
and was it worth it...?
here's the catch:
not only the river but we have changed.

And even as we fight the changes we change:
highly organized cell clusters with minds & souls
lonely exceptions in vegetative world
each cell highly organized structure of energy
vegetative exceptions inorganic world
but not lonely
viral key
crystal pivot
whether we know it or not
whether we like it or not
we are every moment.

Fire on mountain
thunder beneath
fading runes:
let your magic tortoise go and look at me
corners mouth droop
pus runs

misfortune furthers
the wanderer.

Gums bleed mind rots
why search the end
maggot food
did this I had that was no solace god
consolation prize
nothing do nothing can
except try explain it away.

Why try...?
"...to be as young as you
and know what I know now..."
mountains quake worlds split apart
strip it all necessities everything nothing
dry stalks brown snapped off at root
and what have I here
all this out there
slug moist earth
leaves dead log sinking
I alive but know what I know
and am still young and what am I
to do and what does it
matter...?

Winter come
the last temptation
civilization
moon spit
earth snap its jaws
rock crack and bone
suck broken thigh and bottle neck
last flesh shreds torn skeleton
and jackals eat buzzards
buzzards eat worms
worms eat each other
great city
makeup licked from ancient festering scar
the dance of life bristles slow

cackling across the plain.

Black crumbling stair
etherless no change
static empty newspaper grave
spider lair
downward turning sperm and blood
involute the fist diffusing sensual
backward flow
no sign god spare despair despair…

Reveal
green wolves fly sobbing shadow wings
trees howl and stamp their feet
birds backward lizards crawl
and melt in rain
death dies so what
birth yield
the carousel begins to turn
a white horse mounts you.

Mutation
jade pillar pumping
the priestess comes great mother
warlocks chant the flaming circle
eyes burn pelvic mudra
the oracle lives
whirligig of galaxies
vortex the cauldron erect
knee deep in snow.

Eat.

Twentysix years have not left this spot
in this world and out
free flowing
left with but the deeper question
yes:
tomorrow
sunrise waking
breakfast.

Tumbleweed don't know
where it's gonna go
tumbleweed don't care
it's okay everywhere.

I go
terror endlessness the route
shirtless shoeless
madness my weapon
the game that's not a game and only played by fools
the other side
what lies beyond
ecstasy and then ..?
the boat awaits
the waters churn.

COMMU 1

sexual metaphysics & propaganda
a poem in fragments & headlines

INVOCATION:
FROM EACH ACCORDING TO HIS MEAT
TO EACH ACCORDING TO HER MEAT

Demeter mistress of corn & moon,
Kali in tight brown levis,
soapy elbows bent over the sink,
I stand unseen
by the kitchen door,
katchina shakta,
power & incarnation,
mysterious lady of
moon & corn,
I steal over
behind you &
grab ass

O CHILDREN OF TOMORROW

know that once our parents
failed to recognize each other, saw nothing
but the walls of their own minds
& built machines
of greed & fear that turned against them, murdering
their very flesh & earth.

O children, know
that then we children went away
to live among ourselves
among the trees in peace
& there we learned
that to survive we must commune,
try to share all things & love, the men
our son & father, the women our sister
& our wife.
A few
of them followed us. Most others
died.

O do not mourn, mad sensual children,
celebrate
the passing of delusion,
hold a feast upon the gentle hills,
sing of love until our restless mind stops crying,
sing of love
until our warring mind is stilled.

CALL TO ARMS: UNIFY THE FIELD

All matter is in motion,
Einstein said,
all matter is at rest,
each conscious point a center of the universe,
around which a dream of reality swirls,
each particle or wave an energetic void
which consciousness calls a *thing.*

Then why should it matter?
People illusions, phantom objects at best,
states of nothing in motion,
thought forms
like here & now, infinity, eternity,
nothing is left to one but Self:
then whom is there to love?
a lonely place to suicide or pray.
But then again, only the mad
are sensuous enough
to walk through walls.

SEXUALITY

crystal pools
in dark sweating caves
where blind transparent fish
wait
noiselessly

MILK BLUE FROM YOUR NIPPLES

Milk blue from your nipples soft like
honey on my tongue.

my mother's nipples:
darker than yours but
the same warm smell, in-
toxicating.

father must have shared them too,
perhaps remembering as he drank
my grandmother.

breast to mouth to breast: a continuous stream
of milk & flesh in bodies
renewed from the dank recesses of
nowhere through nothing: a
hole dark infinite body
clouds of pubic hair energy
double helix molecule swirl
into plants animals
first woman man is us, primal life itself
still alive, the same joyous pulsating mind
eternal inches inside your
sweet meat universe exploding space exploding
time.

I'D LIKE TO BE

I'm not so much interested in
walking on the moon but
I wouldn't mind being
the first man to
piss on the moon.

DOORWAYS & STAIRWAYS

I sing of doorways and stairways,
trapdoors and roofs;
of the perpetual revelation of
events, phenomena, history, mind
unfurling in time, time un-
furling as mind to four billion pairs
of eyes of the same Self, each
alone struggling to correlate
the infinite evidence within
a finite brain,
capable of clarity only in
bursts through thoughtfield anti-
chaos armor,
clarities which fade
in an instant, after-images
of fantasies, leaving us
in uncertainty again
until whatever happens next
happens & we can go
on.
Thought, unlike
consciousness, is
a chemical reaction.
So I sing of doorways and stairways,
trapdoors and roofs, shadows
of autumn leaves rustling
through the green grass.

ON THE EXCESS AND CORRUPTION

Mind is your breasts slow sensual wobble
as you move my hundred million years of flesh
willing itself to continue,
mind is endlessly expanding energy
turning in upon itself endlessly
like the universe,
mind is the spark in the infinity between mirrors
that contains it all,
mind is the cannibalist system
grinding workers into cancerburger
(over thirty billion served),
mind is god suffering in our own created illusion,
mind is the excess and corruption
of presidential power,
mind is social revolution,
mind is release,
mind is light.

THE SKY BELONGS TO THE PEOPLE

When we finally wake,
surprised at first to see
our fallen vehicles separate from our space,
as through a window to another land
& neither hand
nor word can penetrate the veil,
we panic for a moment.
But no,
we are still here,
whoever, wherever we are.
Then wonder
at this new vehicle freed
& look about in wonder
& finally turn our mind
to what awaits.

OBSERVE IT APPEAR, OBSERVE IT MOVE THROUGH ALL POSSIBLE PERMUTATIONS, OBSERVE IT DISAPPEAR.

Commune ends alienation.
The Paris Commune.
The fall of Saigon
Notice the familiar sensuous progression
as you fall asleep,
like a caterpillar cocooning.
Notice
the dark corners you turn,
the transitions, transformations.
Be alert:
loss of consciousness is a trick
you play upon yourself.
Notice how the dream forms,
what stuff it is made of,
where it comes from.
See yourself in it,
wonder what you're doing, thinking.
Creep closer. Slip inside.
Now you are in your dream body and
can go anywhere you wish.
Be careful you don't get lost.
Commune
means together.
The Pittsburgh Commune.
New York in the Fall.
The Fall of New York

LAO TSE ON THE HO CHI MINH TRAIL

You know very well
you're an illusion:
why the hell
don't you start acting like one?

NONE OF US IS LIBERATED UNTIL WE ALL ARE

The mind struggles to unfold in beauty like
the earth & sky (there are only ends, there are
only means).
Anuhctal teaches
the diversities & the unity:
unclarity is the obstacle is a choice.
Reality &
systems of reality;
politics & systems of politics.
But
the pain of realization is
great. The mind polarized seeks
resolution & freedom from
pain by
destroying the body. We already know
what ghastly flowers grow
in the cracks between worlds.
Nonetheless we
must be born, must invent
a structure that permits it, free
flowing where energy can
stream, we must commu-
nicate again.
No matter what we do,
consciousness in time will unfold.
Beautiful or
not is our choice. The mind
unifying seeks to heal.

POLITICS OCCURS EVERY TIME GENITALS WANT TO TOUCH

Who owns the land on a crowded planet
is famine war & police state,
alienation, exclusion,
devastation. There's no
alternative other than
extinction to getting it
together, unafraid to
trust each
other, unafraid to touch
each other, letting our
head unwind, seeing
whatever there is to see,
being whatever
we have to be,
together, gently, as
families in liberation.

ON THE CORRECT HANDLING OF CONTRADICTIONS AMONG THE PEOPLE

Science & technology study the mechanics
of the illusion, the one in order
to reveal the truth for the truth makes us free,
the other to better manipulate the
illusion.

Terrified of universe
collapse, terrified of freedom, this most
material of civilizations, unwilling to face
the truth, abandoned by our own science within
a contradiction within an empirical
contradiction, without even material to cling
to, unwilling to resolve the contradictions,
spinning dizzily on an arm of a timeless
imaginary pinwheel spinning on an arm
of a larger imaginary pinwheel spinning nowhere
in a centerless infinity, terrified of
universe collapse, terrified of freedom,
having forgotten the songs, the old
songs to the gods we have forgotten exist, songs
of the hunt & the love feast,
of setting the stars in order,
almost numb from pain & emptiness, from staring
into our abyss, clinging
savagely, pathetically
in desperate hope & fear
to the only meaning we have
let ourselves
know: the mechanics, the machinery, the
mathematics, the United States
of America,
to what new toys tomorrow may
bring to save us, what new toys today
have brought us to the verge of

extinction.

According to Einstein, it is no more true
to say the earth revolves
around the sun than it is to say
the sun revolves around the earth, no less true to say
the earth is standing still & the sky spinning.

Commune means
sharing
the air, earth, waters, means of survival,
respecting &
tending the beautiful illusion.
Commune is sensual,
not material.
Communists are
erotic.

SEIZE THE LAND (FISHER'S PEAK, TRINIDAD, COLORADO,1967)

Late afternoon, summer,
a hot wind out of the west,
Drop City shimmers.

Mike stumbles out of his dome,
eyes veined, takes a long piss.
"Mike," I say, "they just killed Robert Kennedy."
Face screwed blinks & shakes his head
then nods in the distance, still pissing.
"See that mountain? Well it's still there."

The mountain, by the way,
is owned by the Rockefeller family.
There's a barbed wire fence around it.
When I mentioned that to a lady from town,
she replied,
"How nice of Mr. Rockefeller
to provide
such a beautiful view
for the people."

ON THE ORIGIN OF EVIL IN THE WORLD

The face of Richard
Nixon, criminal of war,
makeup cracked by a corrupt
smile: a strange disguise even
for godshit.

POWER TO THE KATCHINAS (PERSPECTIVE: PLANET, SPECIES)

Auto accident, ultimate
meeting of man & machine, leaving us
trapped in endlessly repeating
horror semi-conscious between two worlds.

Thank god eternity isn't
forever.
Alienation civilization is choice.
Bodies, I repeat, are real.
Economic equality, individual freedom.
When you see yourself in two places at once, arise.
In the spirit body we can travel anywhere on this plane.
But in the dream body we can travel
anywhere.

Marx would have
understood as he wandered through
the valley of lepers crying love
for the kingdom is at hand.

THE PIGS VS THE PEOPLE: TAKE US TO YOUR LEADER

Thought dualizes, qualifies, excludes: this
is our sangsara. As we perceive the Other, we
invent him.
Thought structures; reality flows;
structure grips the mind with
ghostly tentacles after the reality has
flowed on.

Any human may lead. Only dead men become
Leaders. Watch children; see where the pork
grows & why. To Off him, follow him
home into your head.

The death of a society, the death of a
thought. Thought fades to
nothingness; Mind - like reality -
flows on.

A society that fears to die
delays re-
birth & makes it more difficult, dangerous,
painful, costly.

To commune the body we must
commune the mind, resolve the
contradictions, the one into the
many, the many into the one: THIS IS THE
ONLY WAY TO END THE WAR IN VIETNAM.
To commune is to ease the pain.

WAR REPARATIONS TO THE PEOPLE OF THE WORLD

I used to wonder what went wrong
with this country then I found out
it was built on
genocide slavery servitude and wage-slavery
but luckily
katchinas drive starships
and enslaved people always rise.

CHE IN BOLIVIA

infinity is eternal space, eternity
is infinite time, it is always here, it is
always now, now is infinity, here is eternity,
if we don't do it now we never will. the
united states, with 6% of the world's
population, devours 30%
of the world's resources;
3% of united
states population devours 60% of that 30%.

DARE TO WIN

Those trees aren't dying,
that pavement, those telephone poles
have been here since time never began
and will be here
until time never ends,
even when the last of us
is meat for fish and birds,
we too will be as we have always been:
these soft thighs, this sensual dance,
this pleasure pain,
watching the appearances change.

Choice is delusion, yes.
Nonetheless in the eternal present we have total choice.
At this very instant secret US factories
are manufacturing nuclear bombs;
at this very instant US planes are
bombing villages;
at this very instant your landlord is thinking
of raising your rent;
at this very instant
your lover is seeing a planetary healing vision;
at this very instant
twenty thousand people are being born.
AT THIS VERY INSTANT THE TREES ARE DYING.

1 GRAIN, 10,000 GRAINS

technology is continually evolving
store of practical methods;
a way of thought, its only
value judgement is
what works.

back in the 1960s
rumor had it that
a guerrilla army was
forming in the Sangre de Cristo
mountains of Colorado,
made up mainly of veterans of
Vietnam.

technology is
agriculture, technology is yoga,
technology is how to get
there. Jesus taught
technology. where do we want to get?

SYNOPSIS OF THE STORY: INTRODUCTION & CHAPTER 1

Then long ships with white sails
appeared & light-skinned men stepped
forth upon the wooded shore & met
the dark-eyed people there
with fire & enslaved them
& slaughtered them &
drove them to the mountains &
deserts where they hid
& they died.

Then more ships appeared,
holds heavy listing
in the waves, chains clanking
on black ankles stumbling
down gangplanks to
till the blood-soaked soil.

Now, among the whites
was great inequality: those
rich in wealth were also
rich in privilege & power, &
power bought privilege & wealth:
This was their law.

And the greatest wealth lay
in the land & the people, so both
they treated as property, up for
grabs, to be possessed, exploited,
disposed of.

And the violent governed
over the gentle, the
shrewd & unscrupulous
over the simple, the old over
the young, the males over
the females. And each

lived out his days in hoarding, each lived
out his days in fear.

For the poor plotted against the rich,
the women against the men, the children
against their parents.
But the least & poorest
of whites was still
wealthy & privileged &
powerful to those of dark
eye & dark skin.

And the dark plotted too.
And the land was bathed in tears.

TIRED IN OUR MANY WANDERINGS

Tired in our many wanderings
suddenly restless
remembering our mother and finding ourselves alone
searching wind and cloud for signs
then sensing the direction
we will head upstream
without looking back
and meet in the aspen meadows
that no man owns
in the final hours of night
watch Scorpio sink one last time beyond the western peak
and listen to the sea, one thousand miles away,
rise up to meet her lover
then crouch about the dying fire silent
sharing a last loaf of bread
while smoke spirals colors though the shadows of our minds.
High in the mountains
as dawn rises in the north
and the axis finally shifts
we will look into our lovers' eyes and see the forest
look into the forest and see our lovers' eyes
then look behind her eyes and see the flames
look beyond the flames and see ourselves
we will take off our clothes
and forget what we were and who we were
forget where our bodies end and the universe begins
step out of our minds
through a secret cave we have always known
and drift into each other
together at last
home again
among the animals
washed in the first drops of the coming rain
we will join the dance.

ABOUT THE AUTHOR

Born in New York City in 1940, John Curl's family was a mixture of Irish Catholic, English Protestant, and Romanian and Austrian Jew. One grandfather was a Republican, the other a Communist, and his parents New Deal Democrats. During the winters he grew up in New York City, and during the summers in New Jersey farm country without electricity or running water. His father was a post office worker, and his mother had been a show girl before she became mom, working for a while with Abbot and Costello. He has a degree in Comparative Literature from New York City College. He currently resides in Berkeley, California with his wife, and has one daughter. He is a professional woodworker by trade, and chairman of West Berkeley Artisans and Industrial Companies. He served as a Berkeley planning commissioner. He was a founding member of Berkeley Indigenous Peoples Day in 1991, and has worked on the Berkeley powwow for over 20 years. He is vice-president of PEN Oakland, "The blue collar PEN." His play *The Trial of Christopher Columbus* was produced by the Writers Theater in 2009. His transliterations from Quechua formed the libretto for Tania León's *Ancient* (2009). He represented the USA at the World Poetry Festival in 2010 in Caracas, Venezuela.

OTHER WORKS BY JOHN CURL

Memoir:
Memories of Drop City (2008).

History:
For All The People (2009, 2012); History of Collectivity in the San Francisco Bay Area (1982); History of Work Cooperation in America (1980).

Translation:
Ancient American Poets (2005).

Poetry:
Scorched Birth (2004); Columbus in the Bay of Pigs (1991); Decade (1987); Tidal News (1982); Cosmic Athletics (1980); Ride the Wind (1979); Spring Ritual (1978); Insurrection/Resurrection (1975); Commu 1 (1971); Change/Tears (1967).

www.ingramcontent.com/pod-product-compliance
Lightning Source LLC
Chambersburg PA
CBHW071300110426
42743CB00042B/1115